I0170113

Two Little Boys

Stories about Grandchildren and Godliness

Dene Ward

DeWard
for your journey

Two Little Boys: Stories About Grandchildren and Godliness
© 2020 by DeWard Publishing Company
P.O. Box 290696, Tampa, FL 33687
www.deward.com

Cover by Bonnye Albrecht (maternal grandmother) of Albrecht Design.

Cover photos by Nathan and Brooke Ward (parents).

Reasonable care has been taken to trace original sources for any excerpts and quotations appearing in this book and to document such information. For material not in the public domain, fair-use standards and practices were followed. Should any attribution be found to be incorrect or incomplete, the publisher welcomes written documentation supporting correction for subsequent printings.

Printed in the United States of America.

ISBN: 978-1-947929-12-8

For the first two little boys,
Lucas Jeremy and Nathan Andrew

And for the second two,
Silas Andrew and Judah Samuel

I love you more than the whole wide world!

Introduction: My Two Boys

I had one sister. We lived on the same street as two cousins, who were also girls. We had very little to do with boys because to us they were loud, rough, and dirty. I had no idea how to relate to them at all. In fact, I was a little afraid of them. Please give me girls, Lord, I prayed when I grew up. I just knew I wouldn't have a clue how to raise boys properly.

Despite my prayer, the Lord gave me two boys, and then said, "No more." I was scared to death. But I had not counted on this: Everyone tells you before your first child is born that your life is about to change and will never be the same again. In fact, they tell you so often that you get sick of hearing it and almost determine that it won't happen to you—except something tells you it will, somehow or other, and it does. You instantly know a love like no other, one so deep and intense it nearly frightens you. Everyone was right after all. And it happens even when you have two little boys. I was smitten; still scared, but smitten. It's a wonder the tops of those two little heads do not have dents in them from the thousands of kisses I planted there as they sat in my lap, especially in church.

I had to learn a lot of new things. Like climbing trees, camping, playing in the dirt, and the rules of football, baseball, and basketball. I also had to learn to take a deep breath and let them be boys. Boys are daredevils. They don't know fear and danger is a foreign language. Sometimes my heart was in my throat, but the last thing I wanted was for my trepidation to turn them into sissified weaklings who couldn't handle life when things got tough.

And you know what? They turned out just fine. I have two godly men now who serve the Lord and His people. Men who used to be two little boys. I imagine having a righteous man for a Dad had a whole lot to do with it as well. After all, he used to be a little boy, too.

Now the Lord has blessed me again—with two little boys. I don't think anyone ever told me the same thing about grandparenting that they did about becoming a parent. They should have. It hits you like a train, just as it does when you become a parent. But parents are on the local train, and grandparents get the express, especially if they live a ways off. You see those precious souls in bits and pieces and have to cram years of loving into days. If you get the wonderful chance to babysit while mom and dad are out of town and get to pretend they are actually yours, not just for an hour or two, but for a few days—grandparenting becomes Heaven on Earth.

And don't let anyone tell you the love is any less intense. Just the other day I saw a picture of these two taken from behind. When I saw the backs of those little heads, I wanted to kiss them so badly I hurt. Two little boys made me a mom, and now two little boys have made me a grandmother—the most wonderful role God ever created.

And just like my first two, these two are each their own personality. Silas, the oldest, is a card. He is ready to tease and joke at the drop of a hat. He astounded me with his first pun at the age of three, completely outdoing his pun-master father who astonished us with his first one at five. Both occurred at the dinner table, if that should mean anything—probably not since they are both picky eaters. It was probably a new way to avoid the beans. Being a punster means he is not only smart, he's quick and clever. He is also a budding pianist, which makes this former piano teacher extremely happy.

Judah is quieter, but in that quietness come deep thoughts. He startled me half to death when, at the age of three, he explained the process of adding and subtraction. No, I do not mean that he had certain math facts memorized, like "seven minus four is three." He explained the process as if *I* were three and needed to be taught in detail what it meant to add and subtract. At seven he is working on his multiplication tables, not because he has them memorized, but because he has it figured out. And now he is working on the piano, too.

He doesn't just think deeply. He thinks deeply about *others*. He worries how things will affect the people he loves, and his prayers show that. He is as sweet a little boy as you can imagine, something I did not think even existed when I was a little girl.

Children are truly "a heritage from the Lord" (Ps 127.3). Then they give you grandchildren and prove it all over again. We must treasure that heritage and steward it wisely and lovingly.

I spend a lot of time teaching these two little boys, as is only right. Lois gives us the Biblical example of a grandmother who helped in the teaching process, to reinforce her daughter's rules and values, a daughter who had no other help from a godly father or community. That's our role too, and we can add the wisdom gained from our own life experiences as we teach these precious souls. We also have the opportunity to observe, and in that observation perhaps come up with lessons our grandchildren not only need to hear, but might be more receptive to from us rather than mom and dad.

So I spend a lot time teaching these two little boys. But in the process they have taught me a thing or two as well. Who would have thought that two little boys could be full of so much innocent wisdom? I share these stories with you in this book. I hope it provides you not only some valuable life lessons, but also a little laughter, perhaps a tear or two, and the opportunity to know two special little boys.

May you see your children's children! Peace be upon Israel!
Psalm 128.6

TWO LITTLE BOYS

1. Making Preparations

Funny how you can think you are so prepared and then find out otherwise.

We were going to pack our bag that week, nearly a month ahead, "just in case." But at 7:30 pm, Nathan called to tell us we needed to have it packed "Now!" Our grandson had decided to make his arrival twenty-six days early. So we threw things into a bag and ran out the door, dishes sitting unwashed in the sink, bills left unpaid, the baby gift still "in transit," though I had ordered it in plenty of time for a delivery I expected to be four weeks away. I even had to grab dirty clothes out of the hamper to wash when I got there so I would have enough to wear the week I stayed. So much for thinking we were prepared. Silas Andrew Ward, who made his debut early that morning, showed us we were not.

We all prepare for things every day. That's why we plan meals and make grocery lists, shop the back-to-school sales, and have retirement plans. So why do we so often fail to prepare the most important things, our souls?

I find myself wondering if, despite our protestations otherwise, we don't truly believe. When we are young, we don't really believe we will die, at least not any time soon. There is plenty of time to prepare. The death of a young friend may shake us for awhile, but how long does that last? Let me tell you, when you finally get to that age you never imagined yourself being, you will understand exactly how short your life is and how blessed you are to still have a chance to prepare. "And just as it is appointed for man to die once, and after that comes judgment" (Heb 9.27).

Maybe we don't really believe in the reward. I think that may be a bigger problem than not believing in the punishment. We think the biggest pleasures we will ever have are here and now, and that is solely because we only have the here and now to judge by and Satan banks on that, reinforcing the notion every chance he gets with our culture, the media, and the people around us. If we really believed that the reward is far better than anything we could possibly enjoy here, we would try even harder to prepare ourselves for it. "And without faith it is impossible to be well-pleasing to Him; for he who comes to God must believe that He is, *and that He is a rewarder of those who seek after Him*" (Heb 11.6).

The thing about preparation is you never know when you will need it. You wear the seat belt just in case. If you knew you were going to be in an accident, wouldn't you go another way, or simply stay put? Likewise, we never know when God will call us home. You cannot make a reservation for a specific date, then confirm it with a call 24 hours ahead. You simply prepare for something you know will happen some time in the future, *and never underestimate how soon that may be.* Isn't it foolish not to be ready?

We had an instant reminder all those years ago. At least it was a pleasant one this time.

> *Take heed, watch and pray: for you know not when the time is. It is as when a man, sojourning in another country, having left his house, and given authority to his servants, to each one his work, commanded also the porter to watch. Watch therefore: for you know not when the lord of the house comes, whether at even, or at midnight, or at cockcrowing, or in the morning; lest coming suddenly he find you sleeping. And what I say unto you, I say unto all, Watch.*

Mark 13.33–37

2. Decoding Specialists

Before he was a year old, Silas started talking. Sometimes I knew what he was saying and sometimes I didn't. For some reason he said, "Bear," over and over and over. He and another toddler at church carried on quite a conversation across the aisle with just that one word. But there was no question at all what he meant when he looked across the room, spied Brooke, then smiled, held out both arms and said, "Mamamamamamama," as he toddled across the floor. No, he was not saying, "Mama." He was saying, "There is the most important person in the world." Then he looked at Nathan, pointed to the ceiling and said, "Up!" No, that didn't mean, "Pick me up." It meant, "Throw me up in the air as high as you can," something he loved for his daddy to do.

Mothers can decode better than anyone. When Lucas was eleven months old, he had already been walking five or six weeks. He often padded to the refrigerator, hung on to the door, and said, "Dee." That meant, "I want a drink, please." Nathan, at thirteen months, would hold out his biscuit half and say, "Buuuuh." (Pronounce that like the word "burr" but without the "r," and draw the "u" out as long as possible.) That meant, "Please put more butter on my biscuit so I can lick it off again." Needless to say, he only got a little dab of butter at a time.

Marriages have special codes too. "Are you wearing *that*?" could mean a lot of different things, depending upon the marriage. In some it means, "I don't like that outfit." In ours it means, "Oh, so I guess I can't wear my blue jeans, huh?" Relationships may be about communication, but that does not mean they are about hearing; they are about knowing what the words you hear mean. Sometimes people decide they mean what they want them to mean instead of what they really do mean, and that can lead to all sorts of problems.

Jesus is a specialist in decoding our words. "He who searches the reins and the hearts" (Rev 2.23) can figure it out, no matter how awkwardly we phrase things. We don't have to worry about being eloquent in our prayers, about saying something that might be mis-understood or taken the wrong way. People may do that, but our Lord never will. He partook of humanity so he would understand the stresses we undergo and the turmoil they create in our minds. He knows that things sometimes come out wrong, not because we are selfish or mean, but because we are anxious and distressed. Isn't that when we find ourselves talking to Him the most?

Make a relationship with Him that will calm your worries. Know that He is listening to your heart, not the inept words you sometimes utter. Don't worry about eloquence, just talk. Let your prayers be a comfort to you today, not another source of worry. That's how a real relationship works.

> *Who shall lay anything to the charge of God's elect? It is God who justifies, who is he who condemns? It is Christ Jesus who died, yes rather, who was raised from the dead, who is at the right hand of God, who also makes intercession for us...For there is one God, one mediator between God and man, himself man, Christ Jesus.*

> Romans 8.33–34; 1 Timothy 2.5

3. Where's Puppy?

As a toddler Silas had a bedtime ritual. First you read "Pajama Time" to him. Then you gave him a cup of milk and then his blanket. Then it was time to walk all over the house looking for "Puppy," his stuffed dog and bedtime buddy. Daddy had "hidden" it somewhere and he had to find it.

So the two of them searched, Silas trailing his blanket as he walked. "Is that Puppy?" Daddy asked when they saw a stuffed elephant. Silas shook his head no. "Is that Puppy?" and another shake of the head at the sock monkey. And another at the teddy bear, and another, and another. Finally, they found Puppy right where Daddy had placed him. "Is that Puppy?" he asked one more time, and Silas would nod yes and hold out his hands for the proffered pet. Then the thumb went into the mouth and the baby went into the bed, perfectly content.

One Christmas Eve, things did not work out so well. Silas had already had three naps due to the journey to grandma's house and the various family stops along the way. He was wired by the excitement of lights and presents and people. Still, his eyes began to droop so the routine started, but when Puppy was "found" and Daddy asked, "Is that Puppy?" Silas looked at it and shook his head no. He had decided he did not want to go to bed, and as long as he couldn't find Puppy he thought he wouldn't have to.

After several more attempts, Daddy threw Puppy across the room to him. Silas looked down when the stuffed animal landed with a soft plop. Then he picked it up, shook his head no, and threw it back to Daddy. No Puppy, no bedtime. Of course, he found out differently, and not in the usual easy way.

We can all look at that childish attempt to deny the truth of the situation and smile. Isn't that cute? And pretty smart for a sixteen month old. But *only* for a sixteen month old.

Have you ever known someone who was ill and refused to go to the doctor? As long as it isn't diagnosed, that pain or that lump or that persistent cough isn't anything bad. I am not sick. I am certainly not dying. We look on such people with pity. But we do it to ourselves all the time.

> But be doers of the word, and not hearers only, *deceiving yourselves.* (Jas 1.22)
>
> For if anyone thinks he is something, when he is nothing, *he deceives himself.* (Gal 6.3)
>
> *Do not be deceived:* God is not mocked, for whatever one sows, that will he also reap. (Gal 6.7)
>
> If we say we have no sin, *we deceive ourselves,* and the truth is not in us. (1 John 1.8)

For some reason we think we can pretend our way into Heaven. As the Pharisees who "for a pretense make long prayers" Matt 12.40, we think we can sit in the pew on Sunday, call ourselves Christians to our neighbors, and that's all it takes to make it so. You might be surprised how many have already figured us out because that is also part of deceiving ourselves.

"But we are persuaded better things of you, and things that accompany salvation" (Heb 6.9). I doubt anyone reading this really needs this lesson. Let it just be a little reminder not to fall into that trap.

The world, though, is still deceiving itself. It thinks that if it denies the existence of God that will make it so. Denying God means no accountability. It means I can live as I want without worrying about the consequences, such a comforting thought that it is easy to see why so many fall for it, regardless the increasing evidence of a Divine Creator.

Yet the world can shake its head all it wants. It can pick up the Puppy and throw it back, but nighttime will still come, and they will learn to believe the hard way, when it is much too late.

> *Because he hath stretched out his hand against God, And behaves himself proudly against the Almighty; Because he has covered his face with his fatness, And gathered fat upon his loins; He shall not depart out of darkness; The flame shall dry up his branches, And by the breath of God's mouth shall he go away. Let him not trust in vanity, deceiving himself; For vanity shall be his recompense. For the company of the godless shall be barren, and fire shall consume the tents of bribery. They conceive mischief, and bring forth iniquity, And their heart prepares deceit,*
>
> Job 15.25, 27, 30–31, 34–35

4. Follow the Leader

I remember visiting our children in Tampa once when Silas was still a toddler. He was in the family room, around the corner through the kitchen. Instead of turning right through the kitchen when we arrived, Keith headed straight ahead into the living room. At 17 months, Silas finally seemed to recognize and remember us. As soon as he heard his grandfather's distinctive Arkansas drawl, he came running. Deaf as he is, Keith didn't hear him and kept going at first, while small towheaded Silas kept toddling behind, a huge grin on his face, until finally Granddad turned around and saw him.

Have you ever followed anyone that way? The people who followed Jesus did. "And [Jesus and the apostles] went away in the boat to a desolate place by themselves. Now many saw them going and recognized them, and they ran there on foot from all the towns and got there ahead of them" (Mark 6.32–33). They dropped what they were doing and left their work and their homes because they recognized that what he was teaching was different, that he spoke "as one having authority," yet with a compassion for them that none of their other religious leaders showed. He drew crowds wherever he went, people so interested in hearing him that the practicality of it all didn't daunt them. They followed regardless the inconvenience and sacrifice, even of necessities—like food for the day—so he even met that need for them more than once.

Would we recognize his voice if he were walking among us today? Could we tell that though the things he said sounded different than "what we'd always heard," (Matt 5) it was the simple truth? In fact, what sort of traditions might he discredit among us? Would we keep following him even though it angered our own leaders? Would we follow when our social and economic lives were threatened? Many of them were thrown out of the synagogue for their belief.

If he walked among us today, would we follow everywhere as eagerly as Silas followed his granddad that afternoon, with a huge grin and an eager expression, hoping he would turn around and see us and welcome us into his open arms? Or would we be so satisfied with where we are, or so caught up in things of this world that we would never even notice?

> *My sheep hear my voice, and I know them, and they follow me.*
> *I give them eternal life, and they will never perish, and no one*
> *will snatch them out of my hand.*

> John 10.27–28

5. Special Guests

The kids were on the way that day. Most important of all, Silas was. Keith did not want me to wear myself out before he even got here so he said, "Don't do anything—rest. You have a grandson coming. Besides, he'll just make a mess anyway, so why bother spending time cleaning up?"

Pondering that, I realized that God didn't think that way. He made a beautiful garden for his children. He made everything perfect. It was all "very good." What if he had said, "They're only going to make a mess of it anyway, so why should I bother?"

He bothered for the same reason I did—love. He wanted his children (and grandchildren) to walk with him in a clean and pretty place, a place they would enjoy being and maybe want to stay just a little longer.

So I did spend some time sweeping floors, putting up breakables, setting out the little wooden rocking horse, stuffed animals, and crayons, and filling the cookie jar with homemade cookies.

God did all of that for us too, in a metaphorical sense, hoping we would like the place so much that we would want to stay as long as possible. Yes, I know. He had a plan just in case we made a mess, but I keep a broom and a mop too. So?

Sometimes looking at how God might view things in the same way we might look at them helps us to see how he feels. Sometimes knowing the pain we might have felt if we were on the receiving end of selfish children can make us be just a little bit better. Knowing the trouble we go to because we love our children and grandchildren so much shows us just how much we can hurt an All-Powerful Being. That's what makes the true God so different from the gods of myth. He is willing to be hurt by us. He will make himself vulnerable on our behalf. The next time you go out of your way for special guests in your home, and it is neither noticed or appreciated, remember how God feels when you do the same to him.

Today, enjoy the special things God has made for you, and be sure to thank him. Someday he wants to walk with us again in that perfect place he has prepared "from the foundation of the world," and this time there won't be any messes to clean up.

Ask, and it will be given to you; seek, and you will find; knock, and it will be opened to you. For everyone who asks receives, and the one who seeks finds, and to the one who knocks it will be opened. Or which one of you, if his son asks him for bread, will give him a stone? Or if he asks for a fish, will give him a serpent? If you then, who are evil, know how to give good gifts to your children, how much more will your Father who is in heaven give good things to those who ask him!

Matthew 7.7–11

6. Making Like a Grandma

As Keith says, we are so typical it's embarrassing. Be that as it may, let me tell you about my grandson.

He just turned two. As he sat there in his high chair licking the frosting off his cupcake he quite deliberately read the letters on his Happy Birthday sign, the one that used to hang over our dining room windows when his father and uncle had a birthday, "H-A-P-P-Y," all the way through to the end, never missing a letter. Then he told us what colors the letters were, each one different. Before that he had recited the alphabet, not sung it mind you, but recited it. Then he had counted to nearly 20 and recognized all the numbers. All day he had been pointing out shapes, including "oval."

Shortly after we had arrived, his granddad had read him a book. "See the fish?" he said.

"Dolphin," two-year-old Silas instantly corrected.

His parents told us about a time a couple months before when a friend from church had come walking through the restaurant where they sat. "Hi Mark," they said, and suddenly my 22-month-old grandson was reciting, "Luke, John, Acts, Romans," taking up right where he thought his parents had left off.

Isn't it normal for parents and grandparents to brag on their kids? Do you think God doesn't have the same feelings we do? When I brag on my grandson, when I say he is the cutest, smartest little boy in the whole world, I am simply living up to the image in which I was created. "Have you considered my servant Job?" God asked Satan. "There is none like him in all the earth."

At least twice God spoke from Heaven about his Son, "This is my Son in whom I am well pleased." Don't you know God loved saying that?

When God made Israel his chosen people, his children, he had every right to expect them to behave like His children should. "Now therefore, if you will indeed obey my voice and keep my covenant, you shall be my treasured possession among all peoples, for all the earth is mine; and you shall be to me a kingdom of priests and a holy nation" (Exod 19.5–6).

When they didn't He was just as devastated as we would be if our children did not behave themselves well. "For as the loincloth clings to the waist of a man, so I made the whole house of Israel and the whole house of Judah cling to me, declares the LORD, that they might be for me a people, a name, a praise, and a glory, but they would not listen" (Jer 13.11).

In a Messianic passage, Isaiah speaks of the coming kingdom, the church, "You shall be a crown of beauty in the hand of the LORD, and a royal diadem in the hand of your God. You shall no more be termed Forsaken, and your land shall no more be termed Desolate, but you shall be called My Delight Is in Her…for the LORD delights in you" (Isa 62.3–4). Just as Old Testament Israel had the chance to make God proud of them, we have that chance today.

What would people think about your Father if they saw your behavior and heard you speak? What would they think if they saw how you treated the poor, the sick and the weak? What would they think if they saw how you drive, how you dress, how you work for your employer? All some people will ever know about God is what they see in you.

Make your Heavenly Father proud enough to brag about you today. "Have you seen my child? There is none like him in all the earth."

His divine power has granted to us all things that pertain to life and godliness, through the knowledge of him who called us to his own glory and excellence, by which he has granted to us his precious and very great promises, so that through them you may become partakers of the divine nature, having escaped from the corruption that is in the world because of sinful desire

2 Peter 1.3–4

7. Oh the Down!

Two-year-old Silas has a funny way of asking us to put him down. "Oh the down," he says wistfully with a sigh that communicates far beyond his years. If we don't do it fast enough, he squirms to the point that we put him down in self-defense. At nearly thirty pounds now, he is getting a little too heavy for this grandma to handle without his cooperation. The eye surgeon probably wouldn't be too happy either.

I would hold him longer if he would let me. I would hold him all day and all night. I can't get enough of holding him, in fact, but I don't want to make him stay in my arms. Holding a prisoner is not the same as holding a cherished grandchild.

Too many folks have the wrong idea about the security of the believer.

> My sheep hear my voice, and I know them, and they follow me: and I give unto them eternal life; and they shall never perish, and no one shall snatch them out of my hand. My Father, who has given them to me, is greater than all; and no one is able to snatch them out of the Father's hand. (John 10.27–29)

As long as we stay in God's hand, we are safe. He will not allow us to be tempted more than we can stand. He will give grace that not only forgives our sins, but helps us through the storms of life. *Nothing can separate us from the love of God,* Paul reminds the Romans in 8.39. There is your security of the believer.

But God will hold no prisoners. As soon as we start squirming, as soon as we wistfully sigh, "Oh the down," he will let us go. Unlike aging grandparents, he *could* hold on to us, but God wants a child who wants to be in his arms, not one who kicks and screams and begs to be let go. We will have no one to blame but ourselves if we lose our souls.

> For if, after they have escaped the defilements of the world through the knowledge of our Lord and Savior Jesus Christ, they are again entangled in them and overcome, the last state has become worse for them than the first. (2 Pet 2.20)

You know what? Many times after I put him down, Silas comes running back. "Grandma!" he says with arms held up high, and I will pick him up gladly, even if my back does complain a bit. There is yet another bit of security. God will pick us up when we come back, eager to be held again in his loving arms. It is entirely up to us whether we stay there.

> *Who by God's power are being guarded through faith for a salvation ready to be revealed in the last time*
>
> 1 Peter 1.5

8. Bussenwuddy

We had our first opportunity for an overnight with our grandson Silas when he was two. It was better than a trip to Disneyworld, better than a vacation in an exotic place, better than dinner in a five star restaurant, better than just about anything you could possibly think of. Do I sound like a doting grandmother yet?

When he woke the next morning, he remembered that it was the two of us who put him in the crib the night before and he called out, "Granddad! Grandma!" And there was that smiling face and those big blue eyes under a head full of tousled blond curls.

My one concern that weekend was understanding what he was saying. He has been talking since he was one, but sometimes in a language we can't quite figure out. It sounds for all the world like a real tongue. It comes complete with hand motions and facial expressions and he is quite fluent in it. Unfortunately, we aren't.

The last year he has gained more English and less of his personal argot. For two-years-old, as he was then, he had quite a vocabulary. We were doing shape recognition, and he pointed to one and said, "That's an oval." I hadn't quite gotten over the shock of that when he added, "And that's a rhombus." I quickly flipped through my own mental file card index, trying to remember that one from high school math classes.

That morning after we got him out of bed, he turned to me and said, "Can I have bussenwuddy?"

I was stumped. Maybe I didn't hear right, I thought. So I asked, "Bussenwuddy?"

His little eyes brightened and he started jumping in my lap. "Yes, yes! Bussenwuddy!"

Okay, now what? Bussenwuddy…I flipped through those file cards in my mind once again. What have I heard him talking about that sounds like bussenwuddy?

Finally it came to me. "Buzz and Woody?"

Another excited little bounce. "Yes, yes! Bussenwuddy. Can I?" He wanted to watch the Toy Story DVD. I felt like a successful grandmother—I had figured out what my two-year-old grandchild wanted. Do you think anyone but a grandparent would have tried so hard?

God is trying to talk to us every day. He has put it down in black and white. All we have to do is pick it up and read it. Some of us won't even be bothered with that. Then there are the ones that will pick it up, but then put it back down in frustration. "I can't understand this." Well, how hard are you willing to try?

I have had women leave my classes because "They're too much work." Keith has had people complain about his classes because, "They're too deep." Really? I would be embarrassed to say such a thing if I had been a Christian for two decades or more.

Don't I care enough about my Father in Heaven to put a little effort into it? It isn't that He expects us all to be scholars, who love to put our noses in books for hours on end. But He does expect us to care enough to spend a little time at it. He expects us to be willing to push ourselves some.

No, it isn't all as simple as, "Do this," or "Do that." Sometimes He throws a bussenwuddy in there (Matt 13.10–13; 2 Pet 3.16). But if you really care about communicating with your Father, if talking to Him really excites you, if He is the most important thing in your life, then you will exercise that file card memory of yours and flip through it occasionally, striving (a word that denotes effort, by the way) to learn what He expects of you.

Knowledge alone doesn't make you a faithful child of God. You don't have to be a genius with a photographic memory, but you do have to love your Father enough to be willing to work at building a relationship with Him. Pick up your Bible today, and show Him how much He means to you.

> *And he said to me, "Son of man, go to the house of Israel and speak with my words to them. For you are not sent to a people of foreign speech and a hard language, but to the house of Israel— not to many peoples of foreign speech and a hard language, whose words you cannot understand. Surely, if I sent you to such, **they would listen to you**. But the house of Israel will not be willing to listen to you, for they are not willing to listen to me: because all the house of Israel have a hard forehead and a stubborn heart.*
>
> Ezekiel 3.4–7

9. The Missing Link

My grandson came by for a quick visit recently. I spent a couple of hours preparing the house, putting up the things that might hurt him and the things that could get him into trouble. Then I put out the old toys his daddy used to play with, the "new" ones I had picked up at a thrift store, the crayons, a small plastic chair I had bought for him, as well as my old rocking chair, the one I sat in until I outgrew it.

You are never really sure what a two-year-old will find interesting. Their likes and dislikes change with every mood. I picked up blueberries and chicken nuggets, two of his favorite things, at least the last time I was with him. That doesn't mean he will like them this time. At least I know that about toddlers. It would have been more helpful to have been able to remember well my own preschool days. Then I might have stood a better chance of pleasing him. All of that is entirely normal.

In fact, that is normal in every case. If you could climb into the mind of the person you are trying to relate to, wouldn't it be much easier to understand them and get along? A long time ago, Job said the same thing about man and God. There was no one who could "lay his hand on both" God and man (9.33).

Which is precisely why the Word "became flesh and dwelt among us" (John 1.14). The Hebrew writer says, "He *had to be* made like his brothers in every respect" so that he could become our high priest, our intercessor, the one who stands between us and God, laying his hand on both because he understands both worlds (2.17). Paul makes it plain in 1 Timothy 2.5 that Jesus is the only one of the Godhead who fulfills that requirement—"There is one mediator between God and man, himself man, Christ Jesus."

So now we cannot say, "No one understands." Jesus went through a lot of pain and sorrow and injustice and indignity just so he could understand. Any time we excuse ourselves with something like, "Well of course *he* could overcome sin, he was the Son of God!" we are demeaning the sacrifice he made for us, and the things he bore on our behalf so he could be "the missing link" between our Father and his children. We are saying that he doesn't, and can never understand what it is like to be human.

The Son of God is also the Son of Man. He knows how we think, he knows how we feel, and he knows what we can and cannot endure. He sits at the right hand of God even now, making intercession for us (Rom 8.34) because he searches our hearts and knows what is in them (v 27 with Rev 2.23).

I may make a mistake about what will pique the interest of my two-year-old grandson. Christ will never make the same mistake about us.

> *This makes Jesus the guarantor of a better covenant. The former priests were many in number, because they were prevented by death from continuing in office, but he holds his priesthood permanently, because he continues forever. Consequently, he is able to save to the uttermost those who draw near to God through him, since he always lives to make intercession for them.*
>
> Hebrews 7.22–25

10. Thank You for Blue

Three-year-old Silas has learned to pray, and often sits at the table, eagerly clasping his little hands together, looking back and forth at his parents, hoping they will ask him to say the blessing.

"Do you want to say the prayer?" his daddy asks, as if it weren't obvious, and he gets a big nod and off we go.

It's never about the meal. To him it's about talking to God and saying thank you for something, for anything, for whatever happens to be on his mind.

"Hey God!" Read that the way an excited child would greet his grandparents, not the way a New Yorker would yell, "Hey Mac!"

"Thank you for sisters," although he has none, but one of his little friends does, so he wants to mention it.

"Thank you for blue, and red, and yellow," the colors of the containers he puts his blocks in. He doesn't complain about having to pick up his toys. He thanks God for something to put them in, and that's the one that really made me think.

I wonder how many of our complaints could be expressed as thanks with just a little thought. Dealing with rush hour traffic? Thank God you have a car to drive through it in. Complaining about the stack of ironing? Thank God you have that many clothes to wear. Griping a little about picking up your husband's shoes? Thank God he is alive and well enough to leave them in the middle of the floor.

I thought about this again yesterday when I was blowing off the carport. We didn't have one for years, and sometimes I think that all getting a carport did for me was give me something else to keep clean. But last week when one of our usual summer gully washers came through, I could unload the groceries and stay dry.

Then I came in and heaved a sigh at the extra dirty floor. That happened because we saved enough money to buy a new vanity for the bathroom and the plumber tracked in sand going in and out.

Stop and think today about the things you complain about. How many are caused by blessings you could have thanked God for instead? How many extra chores do you have because God has provided you a home and a family? I never had to wash diapers until I had babies. Do you think for one minute I would have given them back?

If ever anyone had something to grumble about, it was Daniel when the other two presidents and the 120 satraps tricked the king into making the law against praying to anyone other than him. How did he react instead? "And when Daniel knew that the writing was signed, he went into his house (now his windows were open in his chamber toward Jerusalem) and he kneeled upon his knees three times a day, and prayed, *and gave thanks before his God,* as he did aforetime" (Dan 6.10). Surely if Daniel could say thank you at a time like that, we can in this relatively easy time in history.

God is patient with us as we daily grumble our way through a life He has blessed in thousands of ways. You have to go to work? These days especially, be grateful for a job. Gas prices too high? You're still buying it, aren't you?

Maybe we should be a little more like a three-year-old. "Hey God! (I'm so excited to talk to you!) Thank you for all you have done for me, for the things you have given me that I don't deserve and forget to be grateful for. For all those extra chores, because they mean you have blessed me beyond measure. For all my pet peeves, because it means I am able to be up and around and go to those places where they happen. For the fact that I have to work so hard to lose weight, because it means I have plenty to eat. For people who get on my nerves, because it means I have friends and family and neighbors and brothers and sisters in Christ—I am not alone."

Today look at everything you gripe about and find the blessing. You will be amazed—and probably a little ashamed. And maybe those gripes will go away, for at least a little awhile.

> *Give thanks in all circumstances; for this is the will of God in Christ Jesus for you.*
>
> 1 Thessalonians 5.18

11. Empowering the Weak

The time Silas came to visit, shortly before his third birthday, Chloe scared him to death. What did she do? Nothing. Our sweet-faced red heeler simply existed and Silas wasn't too keen on being in the same yard with her, not even a five acre yard.

Then he discovered that Chloe was even more afraid of him. She would cautiously creep out from under the porch when we all went outside, but always made sure I was between her and that frightening little human. What had Silas done to her? Nothing. He couldn't get close enough to do anything to her.

When he finally understood, he thoroughly enjoyed his time outdoors. He picked flowers for his mommy. He loaded the bird feeder. He looked for big hunks of bark that had fallen off the sycamore, broke them into three pieces—one for granddad, one for grandma, and one for himself—and led a countdown: 10–9-8–7–6–5-4–3-2–1—whee!—at which point we all threw our hunks of paper-thin bark into the air, over and over and over until there wasn't a piece of bark bigger than a quarter to be found anywhere.

Then he walked around to the side of the house and found the two old bathtubs Keith soaks his smoker wood in. "Oh!" he cried. "A pool!"

First, he simply stood there splashing the water. Then he eyed an old coffee can and some plastic flower pots, and began dipping into the tub and pouring the water back in and, in the process, all over himself.

Then he eyed Chloe, the dog that no longer scared him. You could almost see the wheels turning. He dipped again into the tub and sat the can on its edge. "Chlo-eeeee," he called in a singsong voice. "I have something foooooor yooooooooou." He picked up the can and headed straight for the dog, sloshing water with every step.

I knew exactly what he was going to do, and so did Chloe. She took off running.

Funny how one simple piece of knowledge was so empowering. When Silas learned that Chloe was so afraid of him, he was no longer afraid of her. But it isn't just the knowing; it's the believing.

How many times do we fail because we simply don't believe what we've been promised?

With every temptation there is a way of escape (1 Cor 10.13). We are equipped with armor that will enable us to stand against the Devil (Eph 6.11–20). We are guarded by the power of God unto a salvation that is ready and waiting (1 Pet 1.5). Our faith stands in the power of God (1 Cor 2.5). We are supported in our afflictions by the power of God (2 Cor 6.7). His power works in us, and we are strengthened by it, the same power that raised Christ from the dead (Eph 3.16, 20).

Do you think Satan isn't afraid of you? *The devils believe also, and tremble,* James says (2.19). Since it is Christ's power that rests on you and not your own (2 Cor 12.9), what makes you think you aren't a fearsome entity as well? The only thing that would hinder it is disbelief in the promises of God.

Our weapons are mighty (2 Cor 10.4–5), far more so than a bucket of water in the hands of a toddler, and we should be ready and willing to use them. Yes, we should face the devil with care, just as we would a rattlesnake, but his fate is already sealed. All we have to do is believe it.

...we have not ceased to pray for you, asking that you may be filled with the knowledge of his will in all spiritual wisdom and

understanding, so as to walk in a manner worthy of the Lord, fully pleasing to him, bearing fruit in every good work and increasing in the knowledge of God. May you be strengthened with all power, according to his glorious might, for all endurance and patience with joy, giving thanks to the Father, who has qualified you to share in the inheritance of the saints in light.

Colossians 1.9–12

12. Not What You Expected

We got the call that Sunday morning at 5:32. We were on the road as soon as we could be, but Silas's little brother Judah beat us there by half an hour. Mommy and Daddy had waited as long as they could, their three-year-old sitting big-eyed and quiet in the labor room, but ultimately had to call a church couple to take him.

About 1:00 that afternoon those helpful people brought Silas back to the hospital, where we sat in the room with Brooke and Nathan, new baby Judah lying in a special bed under a warming light. It took far longer than it should have to get that baby's body temperature to an appropriate number.

Silas, still a bit confused, and very tired, ran straight to his parents. Nathan lifted him into his arms and carried him over to the little bed. He looked down at his four hour old, wrinkly red baby brother, his tiny head still misshapen from his passage into the world, and said, "What's *that*?"

I couldn't help it. A bubble of laughter escaped me at his innocent honesty. When we told him this was his little brother Judah, the one who had been in Mommy's tummy, his little head swung back and forth between his mommy and the figure in the clear, plastic bed, his eyes full of skepticism. This was not what he expected.

It took a couple of weeks for him to really come around, but who could blame him? He was expecting a brother like the brothers and sisters his little friends had, and probably just as big. He was expecting a playmate, but every time he shared his toys, the little interloper simply lay there and slept. Where is the fun in that? But children are nothing if not adaptable, and his little brother is growing on him.

I fear some people look on their lives as Christians with the same skepticism with which Silas first viewed Judah. Freedom, they were promised, but all they see are rules. Joy, they were promised, yet they still suffer the same trials, illnesses, and financial problems as everyone else, even the same ones as before they were converted. They've lost friends, and rifts in the family are worse than ever. They expected people to come running at their every beck and call, yet every Sunday the preacher, an elder, a Bible class teacher—or maybe all three!!—tells them *they* have to serve *others*.

Jesus dealt with the same problem among his followers. Some came expecting to be entertained (Luke 7.32; 23.8). Some came expecting to be fed (John 6.26). Some came expecting to be part of a victorious army and a glorious kingdom here on the earth (Luke 19.11). Very few "came around," changing their expectations to match his offered reality. He never changed his offer—if they wouldn't accept it, he simply sent them away. He drove off far more than ever accepted him (John 6.43–67).

Sometimes we have to do the same. We cannot change the church the Lord bought with His own blood to suit the carnal nature of an unspiritual world—we don't have that right. Be careful what you offer your friends and neighbors. God didn't promise lives of ease, health and wealth, or even a church family that always behaves itself. The test of faith comes when things are difficult, not when they are easy.

The church wasn't what the Jews expected. As a result most of them missed out on the promised kingdom. Examine your own expectations. Make sure the same thing doesn't happen to you.

For the kingdom of God is not a matter of eating and drinking but of righteousness and peace and joy in the Holy Spirit. Whoever thus serves Christ is acceptable to God and approved by men.

Romans 14.17–18

13. First Impressions

When Silas came to stay all by himself for the first time, we were not sure how he would handle being away from Mommy and Daddy. Especially since we were over two hours away, it would have been impossible to get him back home quickly if he was too homesick to last. He was still three, and, though he had stayed alone with us the night Judah was born, and the night after as well, that was at his own home and he slept in his own bed.

We managed to keep him talking about happy things all the way home, deeper and deeper into the "dark, spooky woods" as he later called it. It was after nine o'clock at night and, if you have never experienced it, there is nothing quite as dark as "country dark"—away from the streetlights, traffic lights, parking lot lights, and neon signs of the city. Only once or twice did he stray into the dangerous territory of "Where will I sleep tonight?" in a pensive tone of voice.

"We're here!" we shouted as we pulled up to the gate, wondering aloud in excited voices if Chloe would come to meet us. That kept him happy as we pulled into the carport and unfastened his booster seat straps. Then, just as we walked toward the back porch, an owl screamed not fifty feet away, sounding every bit like a hysterical woman, followed by a "Bwa-ha-ha-ha-ha" before finally settling into its usual "Who-hoo." Silas was up those steps in a flash, plastered next to his grandfather's leg and looking over his shoulders with eyes as big as Frisbees. How could I tell in the dark? Even in the dim starlight I could see white all the way around those big blue irises.

"Uh-oh," I thought. "He will be terrified for the rest of the night." Luckily Grandma had made some ooey-gooey chocolate cookies and that took care of the problem. That first impression, which could have ruined the entire stay, was easily overcome, but I think it often is for children. It's the adults among us who hang on to them.

And that brings me to today's point. We all know that old saying, "You only get one chance to make a first impression." I wish we could remember that all the time, not just when we are meeting someone we hope to impress for our own selfish interests. Everyone who comes into contact with us, anywhere and any time, is a soul we might be able to save. What if that first impression you make is the only impression you will ever make?

I try to remind myself of that when I have a bad experience at a store or in a restaurant. If I fly off the handle and act like a jerk, if I indulge in harsh words that suit my sense of an injustice having been done me, demanding "my rights" as a customer or patron, how will I ever persuade them to study the Bible with me? Could I turn right around and hand them an invitation to church services, a gospel meeting, or a ladies Bible class? Just exactly what kind of reaction do you think I would get? Did you have a bad morning? Our bad moods can be very expensive—they can cost someone else his soul.

So remind yourself the next time you are caught in a tricky situation. Paul told the Corinthians they should be willing to suffer wrong so the church wouldn't be ridiculed by the litigious behavior among them (1 Cor 6.7). What are we willing to suffer so the first impression we leave with someone, won't guarantee that it will be the last?

Show yourself in all respects to be a model of good works, and in your teaching show integrity, dignity, and sound speech that cannot be condemned, so that an opponent may be put to shame, having nothing evil to say about us.

Titus 2.7–8

14. Etchings

I still have fond memories of Silas's first solo visit with us out here in the country. He was not quite four and stayed three nights alone, no mom and dad to get in the way and spoil the fun! The first morning we had to assure him that walking outside barefoot was not a capital crime, but once his toes hit the cool green grass, he giggled delightedly. "I like bare feet!" he instantly proclaimed, and took off running.

He was used to being inside all day, playing with his Match-box cars, putting together puzzles, reading books, and watching his "shows," educational though they might be. Yet he found out there were a lot of fun things to do outside, especially when you have five acres to romp around in instead of a postage stamp-sized yard. That's all they give you in the city these days.

He and Granddad whacked the enemy weeds with green limb "swords." They pulled the garden cart up the rise to the carport and rode it down. They dug roads in the sandy driveway and flew paper airplanes in the yard. They played in the hose and threw mud balls at one another. Every night this little guy went to bed far earlier than he usually did at home—it was that or pass out on the couch from exhaustion as we read Bible stories.

My favorite memory is watching him as we walked Chloe every morning. He begged for one of my walking sticks and I adjusted it to his height. Then he ran on ahead, hopping and skipping along, holding granddad's too-big red baseball cap on his head with one hand so it wouldn't fall off, the walking stick dangling from the other upraised arm, singing and laughing as he went. That picture of sheer joy will forever be etched in my memory. He may have been too little to remember it himself, but someday I will tell him about it, someday when he needs a reminder of joy at a not so joyous time.

I remember that time nearly every morning when I walk Chloe, especially when we reach the back fence where Silas's little feet suddenly took off on the straightaway and his laughter reached its peak. And I wonder if God has anything etched in His memory, anything from that time in Eden when everything was perfect and his two children felt joy every day in their surroundings, in each other, and in Him. Surely, the God who knows all has special memories of how it used to be. Can you read the end of Revelation and not think so?

> Then the angel showed me the river of the water of life, bright as crystal, flowing from the throne of God and of the Lamb through the middle of the street of the city; also, on either side of the river, the tree of life with its twelve kinds of fruit, yielding its fruit each month. The leaves of the tree were for the healing of the nations. No longer will there be anything accursed, but the throne of God and of the Lamb will be in it, and his servants will worship him. They will see his face, and his name will be on their foreheads. And night will be no more. They will need no light of lamp or sun, for the Lord God will be their light, and they will reign forever and ever. (Rev 22.1–5)

Maybe God has recorded that so we, too, can be reminded not of what we have lost, but of what we have waiting for us. Maybe He put it there for the times when life here is not so joyous, a picture of hope to carry us through. It may not be etched in our memories—not yet—but the fact that He still remembers it and wants it, means someday we won't have to count on etchings any longer. Some day it will all be real once again.

15. Ping-Pong Balls

Four-year-old Silas and I were visiting one of the rooms depicting the ten plagues during Vacation Bible School. Number seven was hail with thunder and lightning and fire running along the ground, the robed narrator told us as he stood before drawn curtains. The lights were dimmed, one of the curtains pulled open, and suddenly white hail fell from the sky, and glowing fire ran along the floor. The children oohed and aahed and squealed with delight. Then the curtain was drawn again, but not quite before the lights came up and I saw white ping-pong balls scattered all over the floor. The narrator quickly continued the tale, moving onto the plague of locusts depicted behind the other curtain in the room.

Several minutes later we left for the next stop on our "journey" and, as we did, I leaned over and whispered to Silas, "Wow! Did you see that hail?"

"Yes," he said, and then added, "Hail looks a lot like ping-pong balls, doesn't it?"

I wasn't about to ruin the magic of the evening for him. The point of the week was to learn that God was the only God and He protected His people, and the church was doing an admirable job of it. Me? I never would have even thought of using ping-pong balls.

But sometime in the future it will be time to teach Silas this lesson: if someone tells you it's hail, but it looks like ping-pong balls, check it out yourself! Do you know how many people have been deceived by false teaching, even though the truth was plainly in front of them, just because they wouldn't question their "pastor," their "elder," their "reverend," or their "priest?" Keith and I each have held studies where the student said, "Yes, I can see that, but that's not what my _____ says." Before much longer, the studies stopped. Why do we think our leaders are infallible?

Look at Acts 6.7. "So the word of God continued to spread, and the number of disciples in Jerusalem continued to grow rapidly. Even a large number of priests became obedient to the faith." The priests were teachers of the Jewish faith. Yet even they could see when they were wrong and convert to the Truth. Why not your leader, whatever it is you call him? Instead, Keith was told one time, "How dare you argue with a priest!"

Paul was a man well-educated in Judaism, a man who lived "in all good conscience," yet even he was convinced that he needed to change. He was also a Pharisee, one who respected the Law and knew it inside out. Many others Pharisees were also converted to Christianity (Acts 15.5). Despite their advanced knowledge, they discovered they were wrong about something and had the honesty to change.

God will hold you accountable for your decisions, for your beliefs, and for your actions. Anyone who taught you error will also pay a price, but their mistake won't save you. Jesus said, "If the blind guide the blind, *both* shall fall into a pit" (Matt 15.14).

Don't believe everything you hear. If it looks like ping-pong balls instead of hail, check it out yourself. Don't fall for a lie because of who told you that lie. Doing so means you love that person more than you love God and His Truth.

With all deceit of unrighteousness for them that perish; because they received not the love of the truth, that they might be saved. And for this cause God sends them a working of error, that they should believe a lie: that they all might be judged who believed not the truth, but had pleasure in unrighteousness.

2 Thessalonians 2.10–12

16. Catching a Dream

When we kept our grandsons last spring, twenty-month-old Judah usually climbed into my lap every evening as we sat at the table for a final cup of coffee. It took me a minute the first time his little hand reached out in the air, but finally I realized he was trying to catch the steam wafting over my mug, and was completely mystified when it disappeared between his chubby little fingers.

A lot of people spend their lives trying to catch the steam, vapors that seem solid but disintegrate in their grasping hands. They do it in all sorts of ways, and all of them are useless.

Do they really think they can stop time? Over 11,000,000 surgical and nonsurgical cosmetic procedures were performed in this country in 2013, and we aren't talking medically necessary procedures. The top five were liposuctions, breast augmentations, eyelid surgeries, tummy tucks, and nose surgeries.*

Then there are the folks chasing wealth and security. Didn't the recent Great Recession, as it is now called, teach them anything? Others are striving to make a name for themselves. These are usually the same folks who tell Christians how pathetic we are to believe that some Higher Power would ever notice we even exist on this puny blue dot in the universe. Yet there they all go looking for fame, fortune, notoriety, beauty, or even their version of eternal life. All of it is nothing more than a dream. It will disappear, if not in a natural disaster or an economic meltdown, then the day they die—and they will die no matter how hard they try not to. They are the ones grasping at dreams which are only a vapor that disappears in a flash.

Our dream isn't a dream at all. It is a hope, which in the Biblical sense means it is all but realized. Sin and death have been conquered by a force we can only try to comprehend, by a love we can never repay, and by a will we can but do our best to imitate. Yet there it is, not a wisp of white floating over a warm porcelain mug, but a solid foundation upon which we base our faith. Hebrews 6.19 calls it "an anchor." Have you ever seen a real anchor? If there is anything the opposite of a wisp of steam, that's it—solid and strong, able to hold us steady in the worst winds of life. Tell me how a pert nose and a full bank account can do that!

The world thinks it knows what is real while we sit like a toddler grasping at steam. When eternity comes, they will finally see that they are wrong. Spiritual things are the only things that last, the only real things at all.

So we do not lose heart. Though our outer self is wasting away, our inner self is being renewed day by day. For this light momentary affliction is preparing for us an eternal weight of glory beyond all comparison, as we look not to the things that are seen but to the things that are unseen. For the things that are seen are transient, but the things that are unseen are eternal.

2 Corinthians 4.16–18

*Information from the American Society for Aesthetic Plastic Surgery

17. The Proper Mindset

Both of my grandsons loved the peek-a-boo game. It didn't matter if I hid my face or their faces, smiles and laughter instantly ensued. It also made a good distraction.

Judah especially disliked having his diapers changed, but I found out if I held his little feet up in front of my face and crooned, "Where's Grandma?" he would lie there perfectly content while I changed that diaper, moving his own little feet together and apart while we played the game.

We all understand that a child's perspective is skewed by his inability to recognize any other perspective than his—in the peek-a-boo game, for instance, he thinks that if he cannot see you, then you cannot see him. One mark of maturity is realizing that what someone else sees and hears in your words and actions is not necessarily what you intended, and that his own actions are largely dependent upon things in his life you may never have experienced. Perspective is huge for a Christian.

Paul told the Romans they needed to have the proper perspective about things in this life, or, as he might have called it, the proper mindset. "For those who live according to the flesh *set their minds* on the things of the flesh, but those who live according to the Spirit *set their minds* on the things of the Spirit" (Rom 8.5). Here he divides it into having a spiritual mindset or a fleshly mindset.

He goes on to say: "For to set the mind on the flesh is death, but to set the mind on the Spirit is life and peace. For the mind that is set on the flesh is hostile to God, for it does not submit to God's law; indeed, it cannot. Those who are in the flesh cannot please God" (Rom 8.6–8).

So let's make this easier to see by setting the two mindsets in opposition. If you are a visual learner like I am, grab a sheet of paper and create two columns—the mind of the flesh on one side and the mind of the spirit on the other, as we go through those verses again. Some of these things do not have an expressed opposite, but it is easy to see what that opposite should be.

The mind of the flesh is death while the mind of the spirit is life and peace. The mind of the flesh is hostile to God, so it makes sense that the mind of the spirit is friendly to God. The mind of the flesh cannot submit, but the mind of the spirit will. The mind of the flesh cannot please God, but the mind of the spirit will please him. All of that is easy to see when you chart it out.

So how do we go about telling which mind we have? By the things that matter most to us. Is it wealth, status, money, power, a life of ease and luxury? Moses was willing to give up all those things. "By faith Moses, when he was grown up, refused to be called the son of Pharaoh's daughter, choosing rather to be mistreated with the people of God than to enjoy the fleeting pleasures of sin. He considered the reproach of Christ greater wealth than the treasures of Egypt, for he was looking to the reward" (Heb 11.24–26). This perfectly matches the "chart" in the previous paragraph. Could I do that? Could you?

Let's just say this. When the majority of my complaints about the church are the uncomfortable seats, the warm building, and the long sermons, then maybe my mindset is on the flesh, not the spirit.

What would you be willing to give up for the Lord? That doesn't just mean the big stuff, like your life. That means the little things too—taking time out for personal Bible study, prayer, and visiting; actually deciding to throw your favorite skirt out because you have come to realize it is too short for a godly woman to be wearing; missing a ball game because your neighbor is in distress and this might be an opportunity to reach him with the gospel.

And what sort of difficult things would someone with a fleshly mindset find impossible to give up? The praise of men; the humility of apology; being "right" in something that doesn't really matter; acceptance in the community; a good-paying job; an ungodly sexual relationship, just to name a few, and all with the reasoning, "God wouldn't want me to be unhappy."

It's easy to play peek-a-boo like a child, thinking everything is about me and my pleasure. But sooner or later we need to grow up. The proper mindset will show me the true pleasure in serving God and looking to the good of others. If I never learn that, I will always be nothing more than a baby with a blanket over my face, always blind to the truth of my situation and never able to fix it.

For the one who sows to his own flesh will from the flesh reap corruption, but the one who sows to the Spirit will from the Spirit reap eternal life.

Galatians 6.8

18. I Choose....

As we brought four-year-old Silas home with us for Vacation Bible School one summer, he squirmed a bit in his booster seat, eying the long crowded highway ahead of us and the "boring" scenery of rolling green pastureland in Florida horse farm country.

"How long will it be?" he asked, the perennial question of travelers.

"It will be awhile," I said, "but if you were to fall asleep, the trip would be over in a flash. Suddenly you would wake up and we're there!"

He lifted an eyebrow and gave me a skeptical look. "But I don't like naps," he firmly stated, with his little arms crossed.

"Well," I said with one of those what-do-you-do sighs, "that's your choice. Either a long wait or a nap."

He thought a minute and finally, categorically stated with a firm nod on each word "I choose a long wait."

Five minutes later he was asleep. He never has been able to stay awake in a car, something I hope will change by the time he turns 16 and starts driving.

I couldn't help wondering how many of us look at the choices set before us and stubbornly make the wrong one. God tells us how dangerous the world is. He warns against deception and trickery. He tells us our salvation is our own responsibility so be careful who you follow. Yet even when we look at the choices side by side, we seem so drawn to the wrong ones. They are immediate. They are tangible. They are pleasant. The idea of something far superior in the future seems to be pie in the sky. "A bird in the hand…" the old saying goes, and we fall for it nearly every time.

It would be so much easier if God made the choice for us, if he made the sleep overwhelm us involuntarily so the trip would be over in an instant, but where is the glory in a creature who cannot choose?

The idea that God did not give us a choice is, of course, a fairly common theological doctrine. Yet it limits God in ability and creativity. It makes Him a respecter of persons. It makes Him unsympathetic and unapproachable, a tyrant who makes arbitrary decisions, playing with the eternal souls of people as if they were plastic action figures. That is not the God of the Bible. There are too many heart-rending pleas for us to return. There are too many passages giving options to people in all sorts of situations, including whether or not they will serve Him, for that to be true.

He gave me a choice; he gave you a choice. Make the right one.

I call heaven and earth to witness against you this day, that
I have set before you life and death, the blessing and the curse:
therefore choose life, that you may live, you and your seed.

Deuteronomy 30.19

19. Insomnia

The car hummed along the highway as we carried our two grand-sons to our home while mommy and daddy were away for a few days. They slept away most of the two plus hour trip, waking in time to see the unfamiliar countryside sweep past on the last road "over the river and through the woods to grandma's house."

They played the rest of the afternoon away, digging in the sand, chasing bubbles, and swinging on the old oak tree (the same one Daddy fell out of and broke his arm). Dinner came only after a bath for those two dirty-faced, dirty-footed little fellows, a tub full of bubbles and cups and pitchers to pour over each other. After their favorite mac and cheese, chicken nuggets and applesauce, it wasn't long until their eyes were drooping and they were ready for bed. "The tired-er the better," we thought, especially for that first night.

They fell asleep quickly, twenty-month-old Judah in the "Pack and Play" and four-year-old Silas by his own choice next to his little brother on the twin-sized airbed. We listened through the rest of the evening, but never heard a peep.

However, at 4:52 AM I sensed something by my bed and woke to a small figure standing there in the starlight filtering through the curtains. Dark in the country is not like dark in the city. We have no streetlights—unless you live entirely too close to an up-rooted city slicker who thinks he needs one, and we don't. We have no concrete to reflect the moonlight either. When it's dark, it's dark, and if you are not used to navigating by God's natural night lights, you think you woke up in a tomb.

"Silas," I whispered, "what's wrong?"

"All this dark is keeping me awake," he said quite seriously, and even though I was sleepily thinking, "All this dark is supposed to keep you asleep!" I knew exactly what he meant. Even though we had left a nightlight right by his bedroom door, it was far darker than he was used to, and when he woke it troubled him.

By then Granddad had wakened as well, and he took him back to bed and lay with him until he was once again snoring his soft little boy snores, not much more than five minutes afterward. He slept another three hours with no problem at all.

I thought sometime later that week that this little boy had it right. The dark *should* be keeping us awake.

Even the Old Testament faithful understood the concept of walking in the light. "O house of Jacob, come let us walk in the light of Jehovah" (Isa 2.5). It seemed natural, then, for the Son to claim to be the light as well. "I am the light of the world. Whoever follows me will not walk in darkness, but will have the light of life" (John 8.12). And so, as children of God, we, too, are lights. "For you are all children of light, children of the day. We are not of night or of darkness" (1 Thes 5.5).

Unfortunately, "the light has come into the world and the people loved the darkness rather than the light because their works were evil" (John 3.19). As "children of light" we should be opposite the world. We should not love the darkness; we should hate it.

This will come more naturally if we mature to the point that we don't just *walk* in the light and *not* walk in the darkness. Look at Ephesians 5.8: "for at one time you were darkness, but now are light in the Lord." Do you see that? Light isn't just something you walk in, it is something you *become*. Just as at one time you didn't just walk in the darkness, you *were* darkness. We have completely changed our essence. No wonder we are supposed to hate the dark. No wonder the mere presence of it in the world, among our neighbors, our friends and even our family, should be keeping us awake at night.

All this dark is keeping me awake Lord, should be a lament on every Christian's tongue. Not only that, we should be actively trying to rid the world of that very darkness. "Have no fellowship with the unfruitful works of darkness, Yes, rather, reprove them" (Eph 5.11).

If the darkness in the world isn't enough to keep a "child of light" awake, perhaps he has become something else.

> *Arise, shine; for your light is come, and the glory of Jehovah is risen upon you. For, behold, darkness shall cover the earth, and gross darkness the peoples; but Jehovah will arise upon you, and his glory shall be seen upon you. And nations shall come to your light, and kings to the brightness of your rising.*
>
> Isaiah 60.1–3

20. Wielding the Sword

We do a lot of grandbaby-sitting, not that I am complaining. With this set of grandparents, that always includes some Bible study time.

On one of those occasions, Silas and I sat at the table and made a sheepfold full of sheep with construction paper, cotton balls, markers, and glue. The lesson, of course, was "Jesus is the Good Shepherd," so we also included a shepherd-Jesus and a wolf-Satan. On the tabletop we acted out Jesus protecting the sheep from the wolf.

Not only was I dealing with a four-year-old, but a four-year-old *boy.* As soon as we disposed of the Devil, Silas exclaimed, "Raise him from the dead so Jesus can kill him again!" On that afternoon, the Devil died at least a dozen times. Eventually he stayed dead, but if nothing else, Silas will remember that Jesus can protect us from the Devil. I just hope he also learns when fighting is appropriate and when it isn't, and that the war a Christian engages in is spiritual in nature.

Some of us have as little discretion as a four-year-old. God has furnished us with a formidable sword, His Word (Eph 6.17; Heb 4.12). But like Peter, we often wield the wrong sword. While we know better than to hack people to pieces with a real weapon, we stab our interested neighbors in the hearts with brutal barbs and verbally assault the newborn Christians who haven't had the time to learn everything we think they should have in ten seconds flat. We slash the weak because they are easy prey and instead of sowing the seed among the sinners who need it most, we skewer them with sarcasm and roast them over the coals of a threatened Hell, expecting the Lord to pin a medal of valor on our zealous chests.

Yes, there is a time to swing the sword of the Spirit, especially when the weak and innocent are threatened or when the Lord Himself is affronted, but when we fight just for the sake of fighting, the Devil is winning instead of losing. "Put up your sword into its place," Jesus told Peter, "for all they that take the sword shall perish with the sword" (Matt 26.52).

Be strong and courageous. Take up the sword and fight. But don't wield the wrong sword at the wrong time for the wrong reason.

And the Lord's servant must not strive, but be gentle towards all, apt to teach, forbearing, in meekness correcting them that oppose themselves; if peradventure God may give them repentance unto the knowledge of the truth, and they may recover themselves out of the snare of the devil, having been taken captive by him unto his will.

2 Timothy 2.24–26

21. Walking the Dog

Judah seems to enjoy his visits our here in the country as much, or maybe more than his big brother. Like Silas, as soon as his feet hit the cool green grass, he fell in love with going barefoot and ran all over the place. Since he usually ran me into the ground, I decided that first morning that he could handle walking Chloe with me. I would have to slow our pace for him, but I was sure his active little legs could handle the distance.

The boys and I started out ahead and then I called Chloe to follow. Usually she is out front waiting for me, prancing impatiently, but Chloe is not your average dog. She is a bit of an oxymoron—a scaredy-cat of a dog. She is positive that everything on two feet is out to get her. She is not afraid of us, nor of Lucas, but no one else can get near her. Not even, as it turns out, a twenty-month old toddler.

But that didn't keep the toddler from trying. As soon as he saw Chloe, Judah left the path along the fence and headed through the field toward her. As soon as Chloe saw Judah, she took off running. He sped up and I held my breath as he plowed through vines, briars, blackberries and stinging nettles. I took off after him, sure that his soft baby skin would be scratched, torn, and bloody. He single-mindedly waded on through, leaving a trail of bent and broken greenery behind, until finally I caught up and scooped him into my arms. With his mind still on his goal, he pointed toward Chloe and said, "Dog. Wuh-wuh-wuh-wuh-wuhf!"

I checked him over and he was fine, not a mark on him, no blood, no rashes, no stickers poking out of tender little fingers or toes. So I put him down, this time on the garden path, and called Chloe to resume our walk—and it started all over again. Judah chased, Chloe ran, and I followed. This was not going to work. Finally I got the garden wagon, put Judah in it, and Chloe followed behind at what she deemed a safe distance—about thirty feet. But every time Judah's head swiveled to her and his little finger pointed, she veered from the path and dropped back another foot or two, until reassured that the dangerous little predator wouldn't come swooping in and nab her unexpectedly.

We had gone out that morning to walk Chloe. Judah certainly didn't have the goal in mind when we went for that walk. That's why he couldn't stay on the path. I realized not long afterward, though, that he did have a goal in mind. It was just not the same goal as mine. I wanted to walk the dog. He wanted to experience the dog.

I think too many times we live our lives aimlessly. We just let it happen, and then wonder why things went south. We have no plan for improvement, no strategy for overcoming—we don't even notice the temptation coming! I found dozens of verses using the words aim, goal, and purpose. I found others listing the things we should be looking for or to or toward. Do you really think God has no purpose for you?

> I cry out to God Most High, to God who fulfills his purpose for me. (Ps 57.2)

> The LORD has made everything for its purpose, even the wicked for the day of trouble. (Prov 16.4)

If God has a purpose for the evil people in the world, then certainly He has one for His children. So if He has a purpose for us, shouldn't we be acting with purpose? We are familiar with the concept of "purposing" our contributions, but why do you assemble where you do? To be entertained? Because this group is loving and makes me feel good? Because I like the singing? I know a lot of people who assemble with those goals in mind. How about these instead: I assemble here to serve others, even if they don't serve me; I am here to learn and be admonished, even if they do step on my toes; I am here to participate in those acts we are to do as an "assembly" even if I don't particularly care for the method used in getting that done. Do you see? When I have this sort of purpose, it stops being all about *me*.

Why do you work for a living? Do you know the reason Paul gives? "So you may have something to share with anyone in need" (Eph 4.28). Is that why you work? I bet it's not why your neighbor works. And here we get to the point. Judah and I did not share goals that morning, so we did not share paths either. Are you sharing your neighbor's path, or are you on a better one? You ought to be.

The world may look at how you live and shake its head. There you go trudging through tall grass, sharp thorns, and clinging vines when the path they are taking is so much easier. Paul had given up the goal of status among the Jewish leaders, along with potential wealth and fame. "But whatever gain I had I counted as loss for the sake of Christ," he said. His goal in life had changed and so his path had as well. I am sure his former colleagues and teachers looked with disbelief on the things he left behind and the causes he took up. "But one thing I do: forgetting what lies behind and straining forward to what lies ahead, I press on toward the goal for the prize of the upward call of God in Christ Jesus" (Phil 3.7, 13–14) just like that little toddler pressed on that morning.

What is your goal? You should have one every day, not just on Sundays, although that would be a good start for a lot of people. Maybe the first thing you should do is look around and see who is on the same path you are. That might give you pause to consider.

He exhorted them all to remain faithful to the Lord with stead-fast purpose.

Acts 11.23

22. Playing in the Rain

When our boys were small, on summer days when a soft, warm rain fell, they often asked if they could go outside and play in it. I was reminded of those sweet days last spring when our grandson Silas did the same thing.

He put on his swimming trunks and headed outside, first just running a few steps out, then racing back in under the carport. Gradually he ran further and further, eventually out to the old water oak stump some thirty feet from the house, stood there a minute hopping up and down, holding his arms out to present the most skin to the sky, and laughing uproariously.

He must have gone at it for ten minutes, running back to the carport and excitedly jabbering, "It's wet! It's cold! It's fun!" then running back out into the rain even further, eventually to the swing hanging from the live oak limb out past the well.

But it was still spring and his little chin began to quiver, and all too soon we had to take him in and dry him off.

Do you know what started all this? Pure, unadulterated joy. He and his little brother had been with us for five days while Mommy and Daddy were out of town, and although we had a great time, when they drove up that afternoon, it was clear who were most important in his young life. *They* were back and before long they would take him in his own car seat in his own "blue car" to his own home and his own room where he could sleep in his own bed. I know the feeling.

But life may have made me forget that feeling of pure joy.

Despite the troubles of life we always have real reason for joy, and God expects us to show it. David had that joy, and he expressed it before the people of Israel as they brought the Ark of the Covenant to his newly captured capital city. But he was married to someone who didn't have it, and who did not understand. She scolded him and received this reply:

> [It was] before Jehovah, who chose me above your father, and above all his house, to appoint me prince over the people of Jehovah, over Israel: therefore will I play before Jehovah. (2 Sam 6.21)

Do you see the word "play?" David was out there "leaping and dancing before Jehovah." That's how he was playing. That Hebrew word is found in Job 40.20, "the beasts play in the field." You will find it in Proverbs 8.30–31 where it is translated "rejoicing," and in Job 5.22 where it is "laugh." The same attitude that had Silas laughing and playing in the rain had David playing before Jehovah—joy.

When was the last time you felt that way about God and your relationship with Him? I think we are a little like Michal—too embarrassed to act like God means that much to us. We are too conscious of ourselves and how we look, and far too worried about what other people think.

If I am too embarrassed to show the Lord how much He means to me, I wonder, on the day He comes to pick us up and take us home, if He might be too embarrassed to act like we mean that much to Him.

> *Though you have not seen him, you love him. Though you do not now see him, you believe in him and rejoice with joy that is inexpressible and filled with glory.*

1 Peter 1.8

23. Judah and the Hummingbirds

Judah began noticing the birds at my bird feeders before he was two years old. When he came to visit, he loved to sit in my lap by the window and point. "Look at the buhds," he would say, in a voice reminiscent of his daddy at that age. "A wed one! See? And a blue one!"

Before long he finally saw the hummingbird feeder hanging outside the dining room window. He loved to watch the "little buhds" while he ate.

Then one time when they were staying with us while mom and dad were out of town, Keith told him the little birds were eating just like he was, that they stuck their noses in the hole of the feed er and used them like a straw to suck up the nectar. Oops! Not a minute later, this ingenious little fellow was trying to maneuver his nose over the straw of his juice cup and suck it up just like a hummingbird. Quickly we explained that people can't do that because it would not go into their tummies like it does for the "little birds." He seemed skeptical, but he stopped trying.

The next day we came to the table right after watching the cardinals peck up bird seed from the trough at my other window. Once again the hummingbirds flew in for dinner while we ate. Judah sat and thought a minute then said, "Wed buhds don't have long noses. They eat like dis," and he bent over and banged his little mouth against the wooden table trying to peck. That time he stopped himself, holding his little hand against his red lip. I looked closely. It wasn't bleeding but he had a fat lip for a day or two.

Children will mimic anyone and, it seems, anything. Even birds. Which is why it is important to be so careful around them. Silas at three was parroting (pun intended) me and his Granddad. Not that we were using bad language, but it just startles you so to hear it and realize that you use certain words and phrases often enough for them to pick up on.

And not just your words, or even your actions. Children will also pick up your attitudes—about people, about life, about God, about your brothers and sisters in the faith, about sin and evil in the world—*about other drivers*! That means we must be vigilant as parents, grandparents, and teachers of children in any capacity, because we can also teach them what is right and good.

A few years ago, Mona Charen wrote an article about a study by the National Institutes of Health examining children who experienced all sorts of care—large institutional day care, nursery schools, relative care, nannies, dads, and stay-at-home moms. The findings were not well received by the feminists. "Children who spent significant amounts of time in care with people other than their own mothers were three times as likely as home-reared children to be aggressive, defiant, impatient, and attention-demanding...The effects really begin to kick in when a child spends more than 30 hours a week in alternative care."

And do you know why that is? Because children in daycare are mimicking other children. Children at home are mimicking adults who, we hope, are mature and exhibit all the qualities you eventually want your child to have.

If you want your children to grow up to be godly, kind, merciful servants of God who know his Word, make sure that is what you are. Whether you like it or not, he will do exactly what you show him how to do.

*So these nations feared the L*ORD *and also served their carved images. Their children did likewise, and their children's children—as their fathers did, so they do to this day.*

2 Kings 17.41

24. The Little Eye

> *But be doers of the word, and not hearers only, deceiving your-*
> *selves. For if anyone is a hearer of the word and not a doer, he*
> *is like a man who looks intently at his natural face in a mirror.*
> *For he looks at himself and goes away and at once forgets what*
> *he was like. But the one who looks into the perfect law, the law*
> *of liberty, and perseveres, being no hearer who forgets but a doer*
> *who acts, he will be blessed in his doing. (Jas 1.22–25)*

How many times has the above passage been used in sermons
and articles? I think I have even used it myself, at least once if not
more, on my blog. We must constantly look at ourselves in the
mirror of God's word and then we will see all of our faults and be
able to fix them, right? I recently had an experience that made me
stop and rethink all of that.

We had the privilege of keeping our grandsons for a while,
and had taken them to their favorite eating joint. Silas sat across
from me in the booth and we were discussing school or friends
or something of the sort. He leaned down to get a sip of his soda
then looked right at me and said, "Grandma?"

"Yes?" I encouraged.

"You have two different eyes, don't you? One big eye and one
little eye."

It took a minute for me to realize what he meant. So then I explained that I had very sick eyes (which is exactly what one doctor

called them), and that the "little eye" had needed so many surgeries that I couldn't hold it open as well as I could the other one. He was perfectly satisfied with the explanation and we went on to talk about other things.

That night I looked in the mirror, wondering where this "little eye" was that he saw. I had never noticed that much difference. That's when I realized that every time I looked in the mirror I only looked at the other eye. It has had surgeries too, and it is also "sick," but it has not been medically abused as much as the other. When I made myself look at both eyes I was actually startled. Since I always focus on the other eye, I had never really noticed exactly how different the two eyes look.

Don't you suppose the same thing can happen when we look in the mirror James spoke about? Simply looking in the mirror is not enough when we only look at the good we do and refuse to look at the very sick parts of our souls, the parts that really need spiritual medicine.

So here is today's challenge. don't just look at the big eye; focus on the little one, the one you really need to see. I can't fix my "little eye," but you can fix yours right up, if you are brave enough to really look at it and honest enough to change.

How can you say to your brother, 'Brother, let me take out the speck that is in your eye,' when you yourself do not see the log that is in your own eye? You hypocrite, first take the log out of your own eye, and then you will see clearly to take out the speck that is in your brother's eye.

Luke 6.42

25. Read the Buttons!

"Buttons! Buttons! Read the buttons!" and so for the fortieth time that week I sit down with my two-year-old grandson Judah and read *Pete the Cat and His Four Groovy Buttons.* And every time we reach the page where Pete loses his last button but doesn't let it get him down because "buttons come and buttons go," and where Pete looks down at his buttonless shirt hanging open and the author asks, "what does he see?" Judah springs up, holds his little arms high over his head with a big grin on his face and says, "His bel-ly but-ton!" with exactly the same amount of glee and excitement as the first time he ever heard the book read.

He loves that book and the other two Pete the Cat books he has, as well as the one called *Click, Clack, Boo,* plus the one based on Ezekiel 37 called *Dem Bones.* That week we babysat we learned by the third day to be careful what we said or it would remind him of one of those books and he would toddle off to find it and ask for it to be read not once again, but three, four, five times again.

Yet here we sit with a shelf full of Bibles, every version you can imagine, amplified and not, written in and bare, paragraphed and versed, and now even some in large print, and do we ever have the same amount of desire to read it as a two-year-old who can't even read it to himself yet? He knows those "Pete" books so well you can leave off a word and he will fill it in. You can say the wrong word and he will shout, "No! No! It's _____!" You can mention one word completely out of context and he will immediately think of that book and go looking for it.

Yet we seem loathe to pick up what is supposed to be our spiritual food and drink, the lamp that lights our way in the dark, and the weapon to fight our spiritual battles. We moan over daily reading programs, especially when we get to Leviticus or the genealogies. We complain when the scripture reading at church is longer than 5 verses, especially if we are one of those congregations that, like the people in Nehemiah, stand at the reading of God's Word. We gripe when the Bible class teacher asks us to read more than one chapter before next week's class. What in the world is wrong with us?

This little two-year-old puts us to shame. Just from hearing it read, he can quote practically a whole book, several of them, in fact. His whole face lights up when you read it to him yet again. I have to admit, Keith and I would occasionally try to hide those books by the end of a day. We may not do that with God's Word, at least not literally, but leaving it to sit on the shelf and gather dust isn't much different.

> *I rejoice at your word like one who finds great spoil. I hate and abhor falsehood, but I love your law. Seven times a day I praise you for your righteous rules. Great peace have those who love your law; nothing can make them stumble.*
>
> Psalm 119.162–165

26. "Oh No!"

When anything bad happens to Pete the Cat he says, "Oh no!", and now that is one of Judah's favorite phrases, with his special little two-year-old inflection. The last time we visited, we must have heard it a hundred times.

When he found one of his toys in the wrong place, "Oh no!" When his Mr Happy figure fell over, "Oh no!" When he dropped his cookie, "Oh no!" When a bean fell off his spoon, when his shoe-lace came untied, when his wind-up toy train stopped chugging along—all of these merited a loud and pained, "Oh no!" Everything was a catastrophe for little Mr. Drama King. But at least he paid attention to his world and he cared what happened in it. Can we say the same thing about our spiritual world any more?

I remember when every member of the church could quote scriptures. I remember when we all knew the basic Bible stories. I remember when we understood that Truth was absolute and that our acceptance of and obedience to it determined our eternal destiny. I even remember when you converted other people by showing them that their denomination's practices and beliefs were not Biblical. They would do their best to prove you wrong. Now no one cares. They don't have a clue what they are supposed to believe, and neither do we.

Now anyone who has questions about a statement from the pulpit, about a teaching in a Bible class, about the words of a new song is judged as having his knickers in a knot, as if it were something of no importance. His upset is inappropriate and unwelcome. He needs to "just calm down." He finds himself the object of scorn and ridicule, his concerns swept aside as the foolish rantings of a crochety, usually older, narrow-minded alarmist. Never mind that this older person has seen things like this before and their inevitable results. Never mind that he has the wisdom of perspective that the younger not only do not have but cannot have. He—or she—is not respected, and never listened to. His "Oh no!" has become the expected song for him to sing and so goes in one ear and out the other.

God told the prophet Ezekiel that he was to be a watchman for his people. He was to sound the alarm when he saw the enemy approaching. Those people thought Ezekiel was crazy too. After all, who else but a lunatic would lie on his side and dig in the sand, depicting the siege of Jerusalem for day after day after day? Who else would not speak a word unless it was given him from God for week after week after week? Who else would pull out a handful of hair, throw some of it to the wind, tie some in his robe, and then stand hacking at the rest of it with a sword? None of that wacky behavior made what he said false. God told him that when the people wouldn't listen—and He knew they wouldn't—their blood was on their own heads.

Maybe it's time we listened to a few alarmists. Maybe the alarm is legitimate. At least they are paying attention while we often go along accepting anything anyone says (or sings) just to avoid trouble. Maybe someone needs to holler, "Oh no!" once in awhile. And maybe we need to care as much as they do.

> *As I urged you when I was going to Macedonia, remain at Ephesus so that you may charge certain persons not to teach any different doctrine, nor to devote themselves to myths and endless genealogies, which promote speculations rather than the stewardship from God that is by faith. …For there are many*

unruly men, vain talkers and deceivers... whose mouths must be stopped; men who overthrow whole houses, teaching things which they ought not....

1 Timothy 1.3–4; Titus 1.10–11

27. Taking the Plunge

Silas and Judah stayed with us for nearly a week this past month, and boy, do I have some tales to tell—and their ultimate lessons to share.

The first morning we gathered up swimsuits, towels and water toys for a trip to their great-grandmother's ("Gran-gran") in a subdivision with a pool at the community center. We nabbed the pool pass off her wall and headed down the shady lane with mounting excitement only to find a sign posted on the gate to the pool: "The pool is temporarily closed due to health concerns."

They did as well as they could, for a five-year-old and a two-year-old, at hiding their disappointment, but on the trip home Keith and I were desperately trying to come up with a solution. Finally we hit upon one. Our neighbor owns a veterinary supply business. Many of his products come in bright blue plastic barrels slightly larger than 55 gallon drums, which he empties as he fills smaller bottles for his customers. He often gives us the empties which we wash out and use for all sorts of things. We happened to have two that were cut down to about two feet deep.

Granddad rolled those tubs out to the yard in the shade of the huge live oaks on the west side of the house and filled them with water. Then we divvied up plastic cups and water guns and plopped a little boy in each tub along with all the paraphernalia. As children will, especially kids as bright as these, they soon had a good game or two going, and we grandparents managed to stay out of the way of most of the water, if not all of it, especially those extra long squirts from the water guns.

Then Silas, the older boy, came up with the best game, the one that splashed the most water and got him the wettest. He stood up as tall as he could, and to the cry of "Cowabunga!" lifted both feet in a big jump and landed on his seat in the tub. The water displacement alone was awesome, especially for such a skinny little boy. He usually wound up with his head barely above the water, even choking on it occasionally. Good thing those tubs were well-washed.

Judah adores his big brother. If Silas does it, he does it. If Silas says it, he says it too. Or at least tries. But he is not without at least some measure of caution. I watched as he considered his brother's maniacal call and monumental splash. He seemed to weigh things for a moment and then finally came to a decision. "Cowabunda!" he cried, which was a little easier to say, then jumped up in the air, landing on his feet and squatting carefully in his own little blue tub. Even being several inches shorter, more of him stayed out of the water and the splash was much less. He may have imitated his brother's actions, but he had not made the same commitment.

And that is often where our Christianity stops. We make a good show of it, but the heart isn't there. When the time of sacrifice comes, when we might end up floundering in deep water, it's asking too much. Which is exactly what the Lord does ask for—everything.

In those classic commitment passages of Luke 9 and 14, he makes it plain that nothing can be more important to you than he is. Not comfort and convenience (9.57–58); not family (9.59–60; 14.20); not business (14.18); not possessions (14.19); nothing can get in the way. Then we have one that I had a hard time figuring out.

"Yet another said, 'I will follow you, Lord, but let me first say farewell to those at my home'" (Luke 9.61). We already have several references to family relationships, especially when you add "Whoever loves father or mother more than me is not worthy of me," and the like. Then I remembered the call of Elisha. He too asked Elijah if he could go home and kiss his parents goodbye, and yes, Elijah allowed him to not only do that, but to prepare a feast with the very oxen he had been plowing with at his call (1 Kgs 19.19–21). Surely Jesus was referring to this well-known bit of Jewish history when he said, "No, you cannot go home and say goodbye."

So perhaps it means, "I am even more important than a great prophet like Elijah," the one most Jews considered the greatest prophet of all. To make such an assertion was astounding, and to follow Jesus as he required meant one accepted that claim too. Yes, Jesus asked for it all, even placing your social and religious life on the line by accepting his teaching and claims.

You can't dip your toes in the water and claim to be his disciple. You have to take the plunge, even if it means landing hard and choking on the water when you do. If you're scared of making waves in your little blue tub of a world, chances are you have never made the commitment you should have.

And he said to all, "If anyone would come after me, let him deny himself and take up his cross daily and follow me. For whoever would save his life will lose it, but whoever loses his life for my sake will save it. For what does it profit a man if he gains the whole world and loses or forfeits himself? For whoever is ashamed of me and of my words, of him will the Son of Man be ashamed when he comes in his glory and the glory of the Father and of the holy angels.

Luke 9.23–26

28. Mess Makers

One evening as we sat with our grandsons in the family room of their home, two-year-old Judah found three small bins, about the size of the largest coffee cans these days, and summarily emptied them one by one. Small figurines, farm animals, blocks and other toys covered the family room floor. He stood there looking around with obvious satisfaction, lifted his hands in the air and, with a big grin on his face, proclaimed, "I made a mess!"

Then, surprising us both, he began to pick up each and every tiny toy and place them in the back of his dump truck, the big one he can sit on and push with his feet, until every toy was off the floor.

"What a good boy!" I exclaimed. Naively, as it turned out because he immediately knelt before the truck and began tossing the toys over his shoulders with both hands until once again they were scattered everywhere. Again he looked on his work with satisfaction, then began picking them up and starting over. This must have occurred five or six times before it began to bore him, but for a while there, "Making a Mess" was the game of the hour and he was quite good at it.

Do you know any mess makers in the church? You know, the ones who ask questions in class that are deliberately designed to foil the teacher's carefully laid out lesson and confuse the newcomers; the ones who enjoy starting a discussion they know will end in arguments; the ones who delight in pulling people aside, especially teachers and preachers, and "setting them straight" about some detail that doesn't even matter; the ones who pride themselves on taking the opposing view, not because it is the right one, but because they enjoy a stir. They might as well stand in the middle of the room with my two-year-old grandson and proclaim, "I made a mess."

What does Paul say about them? They "quarrel about words to *no profit*." They participate in "*irreverent* babble." They engage in "*foolish and ignorant* controversies." They have "an *unhealthy* craving for controversy"—indeed they can hardly control themselves when they see certain subjects coming up. That lack of self-control comes because they are "*depraved* in mind." In short, these people thrive on making messes. They live to cause trouble. They even brag about their tendency to do these things.

And why is it so bad? Their actions "subvert souls." They "lead people to more and more ungodliness." Their foolishness "eats like a gangrene." It "genders strife." It serves only to "produce envy, dissension, slander, suspicion...and constant friction." It troubles the new Christians and "unsettles minds."

At least my two-year-old grandson's activity did not hurt anyone. It was entirely appropriate for a child his age. What excuse does a middle-aged mess-maker have? He might as well go play with the babies.

> *But avoid foolish controversies, genealogies, dissensions, and quarrels about the law, for they are unprofitable and worthless. As for a person who stirs up division, after warning him once and then twice, have nothing more to do with him, knowing that such a person is warped and sinful; he is self-condemned.*
>
> Titus 3.9–11

Passages quoted in the body of the article: 1 Timothy 6.4–5; 2 Timothy 2.14, 16, 23; Acts 15.24

29. Illogical Fear

Silas is afraid of dogs. Who can blame him? Most are as big or nearly as big as he is and the ones that aren't have an attitude that is. Dogs have big mouths full of pointy teeth. They roar—which is what barks and growls sound like to a small child. They nip when they play—which doesn't keep it from hurting. And licking you is just a little too close to eating you.

So when he first saw Chloe, Silas's reaction was to try to climb me like a tree. No amount of reassurance that she wouldn't hurt him sufficed. But by the second day of watching *her* run away from *him,* his fear subsided. In fact, he was no longer sure she was a dog. One morning as he sat perched on the truck tailgate eating a morning snack and watching her furtive over-the-shoulder glance as she slunk under the porch, he said, "I'm afraid of dogs but I'm not afraid of *that!*"

Yes, he decided, some dogs should be feared, but at only 5, his little brain had processed the evidence correctly: this was not one of those dogs and he would not waste any more time or energy on it.

Too bad we can't learn that lesson. We are scared and anxious about the wrong things. "Use your brain, people" Jesus did not say but strongly implied in Matthew 6. "God clothes the flowers; He feeds the birds. You see this every day of your lives. Why can't you figure out that He will do the same for you?"

Instead we waste our time and energy worrying about not just our "daily bread," but the bread for the weeks and months and years ahead as if we had some control over world economies, floods, earthquakes, storms, and wars that could steal it all in a moment, as if we had absolute knowledge that we would even be here to need it in the first place. And the kingdom suffers for want of people who give it the time and service it deserves and needs. "God has no hands but our hands," we sing, and then expect someone else's hands to pull the weight while we pamper ourselves and our families with luxuries and so-called future security.

And the things we ought to fear? We go out every day with no preparation for meeting the roaring lion that we know for certainty is out there. He is not a "just in case" or ""if perhaps." He is there—every single day. Yet we enter his territory untrained and in poor spiritual condition, weaponless, and without even a good pair of running shoes should that be our only hope. Why? Because we are afraid of the wrong things and careless about the things we should have a healthy fear for; not because the difference isn't obvious, but because we haven't used the logic that even a five-year-old can.

And what did Jesus say to the people who were afraid of the wrong things? "O ye of little faith."

What are you afraid of this morning?

Do not call conspiracy all that this people calls conspiracy, and do not fear what they fear, nor be in dread. But the LORD of hosts, him you shall honor as holy. Let him be your fear, and let him be your dread.

And do not fear those who kill the body but cannot kill the soul. Rather fear him who can destroy both soul and body in hell.

Listen to me, you who know righteousness, the people in whose heart is my law; fear not the reproach of man, nor be dismayed at their revilings. For the moth will eat them up like a garment, and the worm will eat them like wool; but my righteousness will be forever, and my salvation to all generations.

The Lord is on my side; I will not fear. What can man do to me?

Isaiah 8.12–13; Matthew 10.28; Isaiah 51.7–8. Psalm 118.6.

30. Little Ears

A couple of months ago we met Nathan and his family at a restaurant about 15 miles south of here. It has always been one of his favorites, primarily for their signature dish: The Stogie, a one pound hamburger that is indeed one of the best I have ever eaten out.

Having arrived early, we sat where we could see the street, so we did not miss their vehicle as it passed by the front windows. Keith went out to help them unload and before long two little boys came running in with smiles, hugs, and kisses. Judah, in fact, climbed right into my lap and did not leave it the whole time. Trying to eat even half of my Stogie around him was an adventure, but do you think for one minute I would have told him he needed to leave my lap? Not this grandma. I did have to be careful not to drip hamburger grease on his shirt, or drop a tomato or pickle slice on his little head. But Judah did not think about any of those things. He just assumed he was safe in grandma's lap.

A few months earlier the boys stayed here for several days instead of just a few hours. They immediately picked up words, phrases, and songs. When one of them popped up that first night, I reminded myself then to be extra careful. Aren't I careful all the time? Of course, but these little souls were learning from me even when I didn't think I was teaching! And what was dropping into their hearts and minds was a whole lot more important than a drop of mustard on their heads.

If you are acting in any capacity as a teacher in the Lord's household, the same is true of you. "Keep a close watch on yourself and on the teaching. Persist in this, for by so doing you will save both yourself and your hearers," Paul told Timothy (1 Tim 4.16). First look to yourself, for it is often said that a person learns more from a sermon seen than one heard. Make sure your life matches what you teach in every particular. It is too easy to blind ourselves to things that are obvious to others.

Then make sure over and over that what you teach is correct. Do not ever give an answer you are unsure of. Never be afraid to say, "I don't know, but I will find out." Never speak off the top of your head if you are at all uncertain. Make sure the student knows if something is an opinion only. I can tell you from experience that people will take things to heart you meant as a side note of no importance and they will repeat your words more than once to others, not out of spite but out of respect—they think you know what you are talking about, even when you don't.

And it may not be a class situation. There may be someone out there who watches you with admiration. Maybe in the past you said something kind to them. Maybe they saw you do a good deed. Maybe someone else they respect told them about you. You are being watched whether you know it or not—every one of you! Take heed to yourself!

It isn't just the little ears you have to worry about out there. Just like a grandchild implicitly trusts that his grandparents would never teach him anything wrong whether by word or example, there may be others out there who believe the same of you. What you do and say may indeed save them—and maybe not.

Show yourself in all respects to be a model of good works, and in your teaching show integrity, dignity, and sound speech that cannot be condemned.

Titus 2.7–8

31. Sugar

It must be a Southern thing. We have a tendency to call the people we love after food—honey, honey pie, honey bun, and honey bunch; sweetie, sweet pea, and sweetie pie; muffin, dumplin' and punkin', baby cakes and cupcake, sugar and sugar plum.

Speaking of sugar, that's my favorite term for hugs and kisses from little ones. Whenever a child is in my lap, I will kiss the top of his head every 15 seconds or so and not even realize it. My own children probably have indentations there from several thousand kisses a year, just counting church time. My grandchildren are learning it now. And they love it. I remember kissing Silas's cheek once when he was two and having him run to his mama to tell her, "Grandma got sugar!" with a big grin on his face

Little Judah especially loves the sugar game. The last time we were together after I had leaned over and gotten some "neck sugar" and "cheek sugar," he grabbed his buddies and started kissing them. First Tiger, then Marshall, and finally he even balled up a wad of blankie and gave it a kiss. "Are you getting sugar?" I asked, and he smiled his contented little bashful smile and nodded his head yes

Children revel in the knowledge that they are loved. It feeds a healthy self-esteem and gives them the feelings of security needed when they are out there trying things out and learning about their world. Failure doesn't matter when you are loved

And that is why a patently obvious love is absolutely essential to discipline. If you are the kind of parent you ought to be—setting boundaries and punishing inappropriate behavior from early on—your child needs to know that you love him more than life itself. He needs to hear those words and feel the warmth in your voice and your arms and your heart. Then it won't matter that you punished him yesterday. He will know you love him and will try even harder to please you.

It isn't all hugs and kisses. The older they get, the less that works. But you can still show it with words of appreciation, pride, and approval. Have you ever told your children how much it means to you when they behave in public? How wonderful it is that you don't have to worry what they might do in someone else's home? What a special gift it is in the middle of a stressful situation to know they are one thing you don't have to worry about, that you can take them anywhere any time and they won't act up, that it makes you want them with you even more? Do you think that saying those things might help them behave a little better?

If all they hear are complaints, growls, screams, and great heaving sighs of frustration and anger, all of them hurled in their direction, what do you think they will think about your feelings toward them? Even when they are very young, they can feel the tensions. Even when they do not understand the words, they will know something isn't quite right. And they will always think it's their fault and that's why you don't love them. Even when it's your fault for not having disciplined them correctly or soon enough. Three or four hugs will get them past a deserved and justified spanking. It will take thirty to undo the hurt of an angry, sarcastic parent

The last time Silas was with us I told him how proud I was of him, the way he took his medicine without fuss, the way he sat still in church and behaved in Bible class, the way he always brushed and flossed his teeth without having to be told. I told him how proud I was of how he took care of his little brother. He looked up at me the whole time, his attention never wavering, with his eyes shining and a big smile on his face.

"I love you, Grandma," he said
And of course, I got some sugar too.

*As a father shows compassion to his children, so the L*ORD *shows compassion to those who fear him… and so train the young women to love their husbands and children*

Psalm 103.13; Titus 2.4.

32. Keeping Your Balance

My two grandsons love to go to the park. They love to swing and slide. I'm not sure they have discovered the joys of my own childhood favorite—the seesaw. Back then I was always looking for someone else to sit on the other end, and seldom found the perfect playmate. She was always either too heavy or too light to balance it out, and one of us always hit the ground with a bang. As for the boys, I usually put both of them on one side while I sit on the other, carefully balancing things with my own legs so they don't bounce off the top and I don't hit the ground with a bone-jarring thud.

Over the years I have come to see that God requires His own kind of balance. Nearly every major fault of His people has come with that old pendulum swing—from one extreme to the other. From undisciplined emotionalism to empty ritualism, from faith only to works salvation—we struggle all the time to get the balance just right. "Obedience from the heart," Paul calls it in Romans 6.17. And it has been so for thousands of years.

In our Psalms class, we came upon another passage recently that emphasized yet again the problem of balance. Over and over and over you read things like this:

> …you have tested me and you will find nothing; I have purposed that my mouth will not transgress. (17.3)

> I have kept the ways of the LORD and have not wickedly departed from God. (18.21)

Vindicate me, O LORD, for I have walked in my integrity, and I have trusted in the LORD without wavering. (26.1)

It always bothered me a little when I saw passages like this, especially the ones written by David, as these three are. Isn't he being a little arrogant? Especially *him*?

But, as with all the Bible, you have to put things together to find the balance point. Psalm 130, one of the Psalms of Ascents, certainly shows the opposite feeling: "If you, O LORD, should mark iniquities, O LORD, who could stand?" (v 3). After that, another quickly came to mind: "Enter not for judgment with your servant; for in your sight no man living is righteous" (143.2).

The psalmists all seemed to understand the balance. No one deserves salvation, but yes, we can be righteous in God's eyes when we do our best to serve Him, when obedience is offered willingly, when adoration, reverence, and gratitude are the motivations behind every thought and action, when we don't just do some right things, we become righteous. The author of Psalms 130 goes on to say, "But there is forgiveness with you…" and "with Jehovah there is lovingkindness and…plenteous redemption."

These men saw that salvation was a matter of a relationship with God, not ritualistic obedience nor self-serving obsequiousness, both of which are more about "me" than the God I claim to worship. They proclaimed the balance that would fall before the Lord in reverence and service and yet stand before a Father singing praise and thanksgiving.

And I love that they did not feel required to offer qualifications to what they said. "I am righteous," they said, not bothering to add, "but I know I have sinned in the past, and may sin in the future." They never let the false beliefs of others compel them to soften a strong statement of faith in their Lord to do what He says He will—be merciful. Why are we always dampening the assurance of our hope by pandering to the false teaching of others? Let's strive for perfect balance with this long ago anonymous brother: "With Jehovah there is plenteous redemption, and he shall redeem us!"

Blessed is he whose transgression is forgiven, Whose sin is covered. Blessed is the man unto whom Jehovah does not impute iniquity, And in whose spirit there is no guile.

These things have I written…that you may know you have eternal life.

Psalm 32.1–2; 1 John 5.13

33. Mud Fight

Silas came to visit a few weeks ago all by himself. Granddad had carefully planned the play time, and on the first afternoon, as the thermometer hit 95, and the sun beat down mercilessly, he grabbed the garden hose and I knew immediately what was up.

Keith was always a hands-on Dad, more hands on than the boys wanted in some cases, but also in the fun times. He played with them from the time they were born, carefully moderating his strength when they were small, but never moderating the little boy inside that never quite left him. One of my favorite pictures came when he knocked on the door one rainy day, and there the three of them stood, streaked with mud, having played in the soft warm rain throwing mud balls until you could only tell which was which by their relative size.

So now it was four-year-old Silas's turn, his baptism by mud, so to speak, as Keith filled up the low spot in front of the sour orange and the herb bed, dammed by a berm so the water would back up and have time to soak into the ground before rushing on down the hill to the run just off the east side of the property. As soon as the spot was a couple inches deep, Keith called him in to splash around. Even that took awhile, but finally Silas waded in and started jumping up and down, squealing with delight as the water splashed up around him, and especially when it splashed on Granddad.

Then came the magic moment. Keith reached down into the black mud, scraped up a handful, and flung it carefully onto Silas's back. Talk about indignant! He scrambled up the slope to the carport where I sat in the breeze of a fan, drinking iced tea and watching the fun. "Granddad threw mud on me," he complained as he spun in a circle trying to see the damage behind him.

"So throw some on him!" I said encouragingly.

He was aghast. "But it's dirty," he argued.

"That's the fun," I told him, and he slowly walked back to the puddle, glancing over his shoulder at me with a skeptical look.

Granddad met him with another handful of mud, this time on the chest. "Arghh!" he protested and scrambled away, but this time not to me. I was obviously not on his side in this one.

"Here," Keith said, and stood, chest bare and arms out wide. "Throw some on me."

Once again, Silas yelled, "No," but it wasn't long till he finally picked up a handful of mud on his own. Keith stood there with a grin, waiting as Silas walked up to him. But the little guy couldn't stand it. Just as he got within a four-year-old's throwing range, he turned and threw the mud into the puddle instead. Immediately, Keith picked up a handful and threw it on him. Silas ran around in circles, but never left the area this time. In a flash he had another fistful, but once again threw it in the puddle.

Finally, Keith sat down in the mud. "See? I'm already muddy now. It's okay to throw it on me."

It still took another five minutes, but finally Silas got into the spirit of the thing and threw a generous handful at Keith. I am not sure how much reached skin, but he was as thrilled as if he had dumped a bucketful on him.

For the next thirty minutes the mud was flying. They both wound up with mud caked on their shorts, dripping from clumps on their shoulders, bellies, backs, and even their heads. I doubt Silas had ever been that dirty in his entire life, and he thoroughly enjoyed it.

I could do a lot with this one. I could talk about hands-on fathering. I could talk about shucking your dignity so you can play with your child, about shedding that authoritative image so he will know you love him enough not just to correct him, but to enjoy being with him—on his level, not yours. That's easy, so I will let you take care of those.

How about this? Did you notice how hard it was for Silas to actually start throwing the mud? Even though he was assured it was all right, even though he was encouraged to have fun that normally was not allowed, it still took a long time for him to give in, but give in he did. Why do we think we can hold up against far more powerful forces than that when we place our souls in harm's way?

The world will tell you it's all right. The world will tell you it's fun. The world will say, "Look at me. See? I'm doing just fine, and so will you." If you think you won't give in, you probably have an inflated opinion of your spiritual strength. The truly strong person would have never been there to begin with.

So take it from a little boy who had the time of his life in a mud fight. You will give in too, only your fight will end up with a dirt that can't be washed away with a hose, and you may enjoy it too much to ever leave the mud puddle behind.

You therefore, beloved, knowing this beforehand, take care that you are not carried away with the error of lawless people and lose your own stability. But grow in the grace and knowledge of our Lord and Savior Jesus Christ. To him be the glory both now and to the day of eternity. Amen.

2 Peter 3.17–18

34. Kid Cuisine

We just spent a week with the grandkids. When it comes to food, they are just like mine were at that age. They prefer their oranges out of a can, their macaroni and cheese out of the blue box, their chicken cut into processed squares, and their potatoes long and fried. Forget the complex and strong flavors of Parmagiana Reggianno, feta, and bleu—they want American cheese, thank you. And all their sauces must be sweet—about half corn syrup. True, these two enjoy olives—but they need to be canned and black. A strong, briny kalamata is summarily thrown across the table.

Children have immature palates. For the most part strong flavors are out and bland ones are in. Sugar, salt and fat make up their favorite seasonings. And it must be easy to eat. When you can barely hold a spoon and get the food on it and into your mouth, you prefer things that are solid without being hard and which fit the hand. We would never give a child a fresh artichoke to eat, with instructions like "Peel off the leaf, dip it into lemon juice and melted butter, put it between your teeth and pull it out of your mouth, scraping the good part off as you pull, then discard the leaf."

One day they will understand the pleasure of different tastes and textures. Their palates will become educated to appreciate different foods and even different cuisines. Even the pickiest of childhood eaters usually learn as adults to eat new things, if for no other reason than to be polite or keep harmony in the home. When a woman spends hours a day cooking, she wants more than a grunt and food being shoved around the plate in an attempt to disguise the fact that very little of it was eaten.

But sometimes people become set in their ways. They decide they don't like something, even if they have never tried it. They won't entertain the possibility that their palates have changed, and so won't keep trying things as they become older. When I was a child I hated every kind of cheese, raw onions, and anything that contained a cooked tomato. Now I eat them all. Imagine if I had never found that out. No pizza!

What about your spiritual nourishment? Are you still slurping down canned oranges and packaged mac and cheese? Do you still think instant mashed potatoes are as good as real ones, and Log Cabin as good as real maple syrup? What if the Bible class teacher taught a book you had never studied before? Would you learn with relish or complain because you actually had to read it instead of relying on your old canned knowledge? What if he showed you a different interpretation of a passage than you usually hear? Would you chew on it a little and really consider it, or just dismiss it out of hand because it wasn't what you already thought you knew?

Keith and I have both experienced complaints from people because our classes were "too deep" or "too hard" or "took too much study time." Really? It's one thing to have an immature palate because you are still a babe. It's another to have one because you haven't grown up in twenty, thirty, forty years of claiming discipleship.

The spiritual palate can tell tales on our spiritual maturity in every other area. Jesus expected his disciples to mature in just a few short years. "Have I been with you so long and you still do not know me?" he asked Philip (John 14.9). If we don't know his word, we don't know him. If we don't know him, we have no clue how to behave as Christians.

An educated palate for spiritual food is far more important than whether you have learned to like liver yet. Become an adventurous spiritual eater. You will find this paradox: though you become hungrier for more, you are always satisfied with your meal.

> *For though by this time you ought to be teachers, you need someone to teach you again the basic principles of the oracles of God. You need milk, not solid food, for everyone who lives on milk is unskilled in the word of righteousness, since he is a child. But solid food is for the mature, for those who have their powers of discernment trained by constant practice to distinguish good from evil.*
>
> Hebrews 5.12–14

35. Climbing into Bed

In case you haven't figured it out, I love for our grandsons to visit. My house is a wreck, my schedule is shot, I live on chicken nuggets and mac and cheese and watch either Teenage Mutant Ninja Turtles or Paw Patrol. The laundry piles up and sometimes the dishes, which is a real mess because I don't have a dishwasher to hide them in. I sit by the plastic pool being splashed on purpose and loving it, or egg on the mudfights, perfectly happy to clean up the resulting mess. I help build highways in the ever present Florida sand, chase rocket sling shots as they scream through the sky, throw flimsy balsa airplanes into loop de-loops, and push a swing till my arms want to drop off. Isn't that what grandmas are supposed to do?

I fall into bed every night utterly exhausted, but still listening for the whimpers of bad dreams or the cries of a sick tummy from too much homemade chocolate sauce on the ice cream, and get up and run whenever necessary. Sleeping late is not an option, but who would want to anyway? Every day is another chance to build those memories and instill those values with a Bible story every night, a memory verse picture card, a Bible game, or craft. And then there is this.

Every morning I lie there still in the mists of sleep when suddenly I am pelted by a soft, well-worn stuffed tiger—Lucky is his name—then a fairly new crocheted and stuffed Minion (ask your grandkids), and finally a "blankie" slowly unfurling as it flies through the air like the flying scroll in Zechariah's vision. Our bed is high off the floor, and a toddler cannot possibly climb in without both hands to pull up by. So after the pelting ends, the bed begins to shake and a little blond head begins to rise over the sides of the mattress, little hands persistently pulling on the sheet, little grunts of exertion sounding with every pull. I reach down and pull on a pajama bottom waistband, giving him just the impetus he needs to climb on to the top, then burrow under the covers next to me. I snuggle against the warm little body, the scents of bubble bath, baby shampoo, and lotion wafting up around us in the body heat. When his head hits the pillow he rolls away from me only to scoot quickly backwards so I can spoon him and wrap him with both arms. We are both back asleep in less than a minute.

At least until the next set of footsteps comes in, heavier and faster, a boy whose head is already higher than the edge of the bed, who can easily scale the billowy mattress and bedclothes and who, already knowing from longer experience that he is more than welcome, clambers right on in all the way over me, and snuggles down between me and his Granddad. The game of "Wake up Granddad" ensues, giggling at the pretend growls and grumbles, growing louder with each attempt, until finally we are all good and awake and ready to begin the long day of play again. Do you think I begrudge the sleep? You know better than that.

Yet knowing all of that, we sometimes act like God would begrudge the attention we ask of him, apologizing for bothering him "when there are more important things" for him to do. Just like there is nothing more important than my children or grandchildren's welfare, there is nothing more important to God than ours. Understand: that does not mean he will always say yes to his children any more than I always say yes to mine. That does not mean that there may not be things we will never understand in this world, nor maybe even in the next. But you are important to God. He revels in the relationship you two have. How do I know? Look what he sacrificed to have it.

And don't you believe in his infinite power? I may have to leave things undone in order to spend time with Silas and Judah. God never has to leave things undone. He can do it all, including the piddly little things we sometimes beg for while still keeping the earth spinning on its axis and the sun rising again and again.

If you haven't climbed into the warm bed of love and compassion that God feels toward you, don't blame God. He wants you there. He will help pull you into the safety and comfort of his arms. He won't begrudge a minute of it—unless you do.

I waited patiently for the LORD; he inclined to me and heard my cry. He drew me up from the pit of destruction, out of the miry bog, and set my feet upon a rock, making my steps secure. He put a new song in my mouth, a song of praise to our God. Many will see and fear, and put their trust in the LORD.

Psalm 40.1–3

36. The Return of the Stick Man

The mind of a child is an amazing thing. It processes and stores information like a computer, tons of it every day as he learns how to communicate, how to get along with others, how to quantify, how to adapt. And he learns these things much faster than we seem to realize. Trust me, your child knows when you are happy with him and when you are not before he is a year old, and he knows how to get exactly what he wants—he will train you far better than you will train him if you aren't careful.

Although I taught all ages of piano and voice students, my Bible class teaching gradually shifted till I was teaching the middle school class most of the time. I forgot some of the techniques I had used so long ago when my own boys were toddlers. Then Silas came to visit during Vacation Bible School and they sent him back to us with a memory verse, the wording of which I knew immediately would be difficult for a preschooler: "See what manner of love the father has given to us that we should be called children of God" (1 John 3.1).

Just repeating this three or four times was not going to get it done. Then I remembered the old memory verse cards I used to make for the toddler class. You turn the memory verse into something resembling a rebus, a picture puzzle, substituting drawings for certain words. I developed my own "ethics" though. I never used what I call text language. No number 4 for the word "for" and no homonyms. That would only make the verse harder for them to comprehend, which was the ultimate goal.

That leads me to an important aside. Some people are convinced that small children cannot memorize; some are even convinced that memory verses are overrated. Small children cannot memorize? Have you ever heard a two-year-old recite word for word an entire scene from a Disney movie? Have you ever accidentally misread their favorite book only to have them say, "No! It goes like this…" and then proceed to finish the page for you?

Just because it's scripture doesn't mean they can't do it. Josephus says of the Jews that their children were "nourished up in the laws from their infancy." Edersheim says in *Sketches of Jewish Social Life* that in the time of Christ, home teaching began when the child was three, and then at five he started the book of Leviticus! What a way to begin. As far as memory verses being overrated, I don't know what I would do without the verses that were implanted in both my head and heart from the time I can remember. They rise up when I need them, and have gotten me through a number of tough situations. How can anyone say that having the word of God instantly spring to your lips and your mind is overrated?

As for these memory verse cards, Silas loved them. Even though he couldn't read them, he carefully pointed out word for word, using the pictures to jog his memory. Whenever I pulled it out he asked, "Can I hold it?" and was thrilled to show others how he could say his memory verse. Then Judah came along and he was no different. He could recite long verses with huge words in them as early as 4, just like his brother did, and he was thrilled to "show off." In fact, when we were choosing verses at random, he got a special thrill out of reciting one longer than his older brother's! Isn't that the kind of reaction you want from your children as they learn the word of God?

So how do you make these memory verse cards? Get out your pencils and let's try a few things. But before you do, let me add this—you do not have to be an artist. The only one who is worried about what those drawings look like is you. Once the child knows what they are, he uses them like other people use mnemonics—to help him remember. And this is where the good old stick man comes into play.

I cannot draw. I can't even do a Jackson Pollock splatter. Oh, I can do the basic tree—a brown stick with a fluffy green cloud on top. I can do a light bulb, which comes in handy every time you come across the word "light" in a verse. I can do the daisy on a stem with two leaves and the square house with two windows and a door. For a sheep, I can draw yet another fluffy cloud, this one white, with four stick legs, and a head and tail.

No, I can't do much in the way of drawing—but I can make a stick man do practically anything. He can pray, he can kneel, he can run, he can walk, he can fish (*I will make you fishers of men*), he can sleep, he can shout, he can talk or preach or sing or any other sound, simply by drawing him an open mouth. You tell the children what he is doing—trust me, they will remember.

One other thing: make important words look special. Always put God or Lord or Spirit in a puffy cloud. Draw only the bottom half of a cloud and write "Heaven" in it when you need that word. Take words like faith and grace and good and evil, put them in all caps and box them in an appropriate color, like blue for good and red for evil. Before long, those children who are "too young to learn anything" will actually start to recognize those special words.

So what did I do with that hard memory verse Silas brought home? Remember as you read the verse below, the drawings replace one word or phrase; you don't write the words under the drawing. What I drew ended up like this (the brackets are the pictures I drew instead of the word or phrase immediately preceding them):

See [Stick man with hand above his eyes as if he is looking off in the distance] *what kind of love* [heart] *the FATHER* (in a cloud) *has given to us* [three stick men, one handing something to two others] *that we should be called* [stick man with hands around his mouth and flared out lines coming from his mouth] *children* [several smaller stick people] *of GOD* (in a cloud).

Silas learned that verse in one afternoon, and he loved that card. If he could learn that one, what's to stop him from simple things like "You are the light of the world, a city set on a hill?" Come on now, you can draw that one yourself, right?

One more step remains in this process. Eventually you should reach the point that you can draw only one or two of the pictures from that card onto a smaller one, like an index card. Then use it like a flashcard. When your child sees it, he or she should automatically spout out the longer verse. It will happen, I promise. As you add verses, you constantly go over the old ones using only the small "one picture" flashcards. I used to have the parents come into the class after services at the end of every quarter. When they saw their two and three-year-olds quoting ten or eleven memory verses just from looking at a simple line drawing, or a good old stick man, on an index card, they were amazed.

Your child can do it too. I know it, and so does God.

Only take care, and keep your soul diligently, lest you forget the things that your eyes have seen, and lest they depart from your heart all the days of your life. **Make them known to your children** *and your children's children.*

Blow the trumpet in Zion; consecrate a fast; call a solemn assembly; gather the people. Consecrate the congregation; assemble the elders; gather the children, even nursing infants. Let the bridegroom leave his room, and the bride her chamber. … Tell your children of it, and let your children tell their children, and their children to another generation.

Deuteronomy 4.9; Joel 2.15–16; 1.3.

37. School Days

I could hardly believe it when Silas reached kindergarten age. How in the world had that happened so quickly? When he found out he had to go back the second week, he said, "You mean I have to go *again?!*"

"Yes," his mother told him, "there is a lot to learn."

"But I already learned," he said, sure that now he would get to stay home with her and his little brother. Of course, he found out otherwise quickly.

I know that no one would say it out loud, but sometimes I get the feeling some of my brothers and sisters have the same attitude. "I already learned!" which is supposed to justify their never studying for a Bible class, never attending an extra Bible study, never darkening the meetinghouse doors for anything but the Lord's Supper, as if it were a magic potion that would save them that week regardless of anything else they did. What they have "learned" are usually the pet scriptures, the catchphrases, the simplistic theories that try to explain away the profound depth of the Scriptures—all those things that smack so much of a denominational mindset.

I have amazing women in my Bible classes, and let me tell you, most of them are neither young nor new Christians. These are women of a certain age, as we often say, who have sat on pews for longer than many others have been alive, yet they see the value in learning still more.

And that does not necessarily mean learning something new. Sometimes the learning has more to do with a deeper comprehension, uncovering another level of wisdom, or an additional way of applying a fact to one's life, leading to a changed behavior or attitude. When I see someone in their later years actually change their lives because of a discovery made in Bible class, I am reminded yet again of the power of the Word. The most amazing thing about this living and active Word, is that if you are not blinded by self-satisfaction, every time you study it you can see something new. It's like peeling an onion—you keep finding another layer underneath.

You may have "already learned" a great many things, but if that is your attitude, you will never grow beyond the boundaries you have placed upon yourself with that notion. Like a kindergartner who has learned his letters and numbers, you will be stuck in the basics, the "first principles," and never come to a fuller comprehension of the magnitude of God's wisdom and His plan for you. If you are still deciding how long to keep a preacher based upon how much you "enjoy" his preaching and how many times he visited you in the hospital, if you are mouthing things like "I never heard of such a thing" or "I am (or am not) comfortable with that," with not a scripture reference in sight, you still have a long way to go.

God wants meat-eaters at His banquet. That means you need to chew a little harder and longer. Yes, it takes time away from recess to sit in class and learn some more. Yes, you have to process some new information which may not be as comfortable as you are used to. Your brain may even ache a little, but that is how you learn, by stretching those mental muscles instead of vegetating on the pew.

You may think you have "already learned," but I bet you even my kindergartner grandson figured out very shortly that there was a whole lot more he needed to know. He's a pretty smart kid. How about you?

106 | *Two Little Boys*

Whom will he teach knowledge? and whom will he make to understand the message? them that are weaned from the milk.

Wherefore leaving the doctrine of the first principles of Christ, let us press on unto perfection

Isaiah 28.9; Hebrews 6.1

38. "I Got Purple!"

We did some more babysitting last month, and the first afternoon that we picked up Silas from kindergarten, he came rushing out to the car shouting, "I got purple! I got purple!"

In his school every child starts the day on green, and his behavior moves him either up the color chart to blue and ultimately purple, or down the chart to yellow, orange, or red. Red means mom and dad have to come in for a serious talk. Usually all the obedient, well-behaved students end up on blue, and everyone is perfectly satisfied with it. But purple? Purple takes something extra-special. It is the height of achievement for a student. No wonder he came out running, shouting, and grinning a smile as wide as our windshield as we watched him through it.

Why is it that I can't have the same glee, the same sense of accomplishment and exhilaration when I overcome a temptation or grow out of a bad attitude? Why don't we all come running to share the good news with one another? I'll tell you why—because we are a bunch of judgmental grumps, that's why. Two things are going to happen if anyone opens his mouth about these things.

First, someone is going to gasp and whisper to another, "You mean he has trouble with *that* sin?" We can't share our accomplishments when we are afraid people will look down on us, will lose respect for us, and will probably gossip about us at the first chance they get. "Did you hear about so-and-so? Did you know he has these problems?"

Second, someone else will puff out his chest and say, "Tsk, tsk. *Let him who thinks he stands take heed lest he fall!*" We can't share our successes without someone thinking they have to knock us down a peg because of our "pride," as they so hastily judge it.

In both of these cases, shame, shame, shame on us! Those are unscriptural, even sinful attitudes. Gossip, which is nothing less than slander, is included in that horrible list of sins at the end of Romans 1. And what in the world do we think it means to "Encourage one another?" It means when a pat on the back has been earned, give it! Don't hoard it with the self-righteous notion that we are doing what is best for the person's soul—"wouldn't want him to get the big head." Would you do that with your children? Would you never praise them for their successes, but only criticize their mistakes?

AA doesn't do it, and God doesn't do that either. "And the Lord said to Satan, "Have you considered my servant Job, that there is none like him on the earth, a blameless and upright man, who fears God and turns away from evil?" (Job 1.8).

The Psalms are full of statements by people of God who *know* they have done right. "The Lord dealt with me according to my righteousness; according to the cleanness of my hands he rewarded me. For I have kept the ways of the Lord, and have not wickedly departed from my God. For all his rules were before me, and his statutes I did not put away from me. I was blameless before him, and I kept myself from my guilt. So the Lord has rewarded me according to my righteousness, according to the cleanness of my hands in his sight" (Ps 18.20–24).

Don't tell me it's because the Old Testament people did not understand grace and were all about "earning" their salvation by keeping the Law. "Do not say in your heart, after the Lord your God has thrust them out before you, 'It is because of my righteousness that the Lord has brought me in to possess this land,' whereas it is because of the wickedness of these nations that the

LORD is driving them out before you. Not because of your righteousness or the uprightness of your heart…" (Deut 9.4–5). "O my God, incline your ear and hear. Open your eyes and see our desolations, and the city that is called by your name. For we do not present our pleas before you because of our righteousness, but because of your great mercy" (Dan 9.18).

Those people knew they had not earned God's love and mercy, but they also knew when they had done well in keeping His commandments. Why do we think it's a sin to recognize that? The apostles didn't. "I have fought the good fight, I have finished the race, I have kept the faith. Henceforth there is laid up for me the crown of righteousness, which the Lord, the righteous judge, will award to me on that Day, and not only to me but also to all who have loved his appearing" (2 Tim 4.7–8).

When my grandson came running out that day I could easily have told the difference between arrogance and joy. Why can't we tell the same thing about one another? Why can't we share victories over Satan and expect others will be just as happy about it as we are? God wanted us to *know* we are saved; he wanted us to be confident in our destiny. "I write these things to you who believe in the name of the Son of God that you may know that you have eternal life" (1 John 5.13).

I'll tell you this, if we are going to "become as little children" and so inherit the kingdom of heaven, we had better stop acting like peevish, petty grown-ups. With that sort of behavior we will never be able to run down the streets of Heaven shouting, "I got purple!"

Let them shout for joy, and be glad, that favor my righteous cause: Yea, let them say continually, Jehovah be magnified, Who hath pleasure in the prosperity of his servant.

Psalm 35.27

39. Drop One, Drop Two

The last time we went to visit, four-year-old Judah made up a game. He had a pile of "buddies" (mainly stuffed animals) and picked up two. These he carefully carried behind his back as he walked across the floor. As he reached what must have been a predetermined point in his little mind, he suddenly dropped the two buddies, one at a time.

"Drop one, drop two," he said. Then he turned around and looked. Number two was placed in a "keep" pile, while number one was discarded across the room. Then he picked up two more and did it again. Before long he had two piles, each half the size of the one he began with. Then he started the process all over again with the "keep" pile, adding yet more to the discard pile and leaving a smaller "keep" pile. He did this several times until he had finally whittled it down to two buddies. When he finished, he looked at the buddy who had "won" the game—the final "drop two" buddy. He was not entirely pleased, so he gathered all the buddies from both piles together and started over again.

This time, instead of carrying the buddies behind his back where, I suppose, he couldn't always remember which hand held what, he carried them in front of him. He could see exactly who he was dropping when. Occasionally he even hesitated before deciding which to drop first, the buddy which would then be discarded altogether. Because he could see what he was doing, he was happy with the end result, which was Lucky the Tiger, his favorite. Obviously, he had rigged the game.

I began thinking about how he had made his choices. If one was his brother's buddy and the other was his, his brother's was the first to go to the discard pile. If one were a newer buddy, and the other an old favorite, the newer one fell victim to "Drop one." Once he had culled it down to only his old favorites, life became a little more difficult. In fact, the third time through the game, Leo the blankie actually displaced Lucky the Tiger.

Now let's put feet on this little story. Do we ever do the same thing? Yes, we adults have been known to determine Truth not by what the scripture says but by who says it. Did Brother Big Name Preacher say this, or some poor old nobody you never heard of? Did my best friend in the congregation take this side and the guy I can hardly tolerate take the other? Is this the view my blood family takes while someone I am not related to takes that one?

Or maybe we make our choices based on how it affects us. Would this view mean I need to admit wrong and change my life and that other one leave me to live as I want to? Would it mean that my parents died in sin and I just can't bear to think such a thing? Would it mean I need to disfellowship my good friends? Would it mean my children are no longer considered faithful Christians, so I just won't consider the possibility that this scripture actually means that at all. I've known more than one preacher whose views on divorce and remarriage changed when family was suddenly involved. Honestly considering the scriptures with rational, logical thought had nothing to do with it.

Our first allegiance is supposed to be to God and His revealed Word, not family, not best friends, not famous people or those with more wealth or status. We are not four years old. We are supposed to have matured enough to make the hard decisions regardless the fallout. "Drop one, drop two" is not a meaningless game with God. He watches who and what you drop and why. He knows how to play the game too, and He will not let His love for sinners influence His decisions about who to drop first if they refuse the Truth.

> *Whoever loves father or mother more than me is not worthy of me, and whoever loves son or daughter more than me is not worthy of me.*

> *If anyone comes to me and does not hate his own father and mother and wife and children and brothers and sisters, yes, and even his own life, he cannot be my disciple.*

> Matthew 10.37; Luke 14.26

40. Letting Lucky Pray

Is there anything more satisfying for a grandparent than being allowed to babysit for several days while Mom and Dad are out of town? Absolutely not. It may wear me out, but it's a good kind of tired, the very best in fact.

Four-year-old Judah has a stuffed tiger he has lugged around since he could carry anything. It started out about the same size as he was at birth, but seems to have suffered a little stuffing-porosis. He is limper and his body parts seem a bit more disjointed, as if someone had hugged on him for years, mashing him into whatever odd posture it took for him to lie cheek to cheek with a loving little towhead. He is still cute—a long head at least half the size of his body with a cartoon-dufus face and a big black nose. His stripes these days are a little more pale yellow and gray than orange and black, but there is no mistaking what he is: a four-year-old's favorite "buddy."

Sometime this past year, the tiger got a name—Lucky. Lucky makes it out of the bed every morning and though he is often cast aside as his small master plays during the day, he always makes it back to bed. And for some reason, he makes it to the table too.

When we were there this past babysitting stint, as we joined hands to pray over our meal, Lucky, for the first time, had his paw held too. Judah very carefully held on to one paw and laid Lucky out across the large table so his Granddad could grasp the other paw and complete the circle. "Ah," I thought. "Something in that little four-year-old mind has changed.

If you pooh-pooh your child's favorite buddy, you are missing something important. I may not be a child psychologist, but I did have my own imaginary friends when I was growing up, so I know a thing or two about this. Those imaginary friends are anything but imaginary to your little one. They are best friends. They protect. They comfort. They listen. They even talk. Why, Lucky even played a hand of "Go Fish" while we were there. This is your child's first close relationship with someone not family. He is learning what it means to be a friend, to be loyal, and to love as friends love. So when something becomes important to your child, he wants to share it with that special friend.

Because Judah sees us praying, because he sees his mom and dad pray, because he sees a room full of friendly faces praying every week, he has learned that praying is important. What concept does he have of God at this age? Probably the usual, "God made me-God loves me" impression that most toddlers who have been to church since they were born have. That doesn't matter. What does matter is that he wants to share his understanding with his special friend. It is a normal part of his life, his little brain is thinking, so naturally Lucky would want to do this too. If he can play Go Fish, certainly he can pray.

"It's a normal part of his life." That is important. Your child should see you interacting with God on a daily basis—in prayer, in study, in family discussions, in decisions you make. That is how you instill faith in him. If he grows up seeing these things, more than likely, he will do them too. And since he believes his little friend can do exactly what he can do, letting Lucky pray will validate in his little mind—even though he has no idea what those words mean—both his relationship with his friend Lucky and his relationship with God. If you disregard Lucky, whom he can see, how in the world can you expect him to believe in a God he doesn't yet know how to see? Letting Lucky pray will make God become as real to him as Lucky already has, and eventually, the only real one of the two.

And it may all start if you just reach your hand out and grasp a well-loved paw over the dinner table.

> *But the steadfast love of the* LORD *is from everlasting to everlasting on those who fear him, and his righteousness to children's children.*

Psalm 103.17

41. The Scooters

For their seventh and fourth birthdays, which we celebrated together, we gave our grandsons scooters. They were small scooters, starter scooters, I called them, about like a skateboard with a handle. But they were thrilled. If ever we got a gift right, we seem to have that time. Before long they were zooming around like little speed demons.

Of course, four-year-old Judah was not quite up to his older brother's antics. He tried his best to follow him in the same places, at the same speed, and usually wound up losing it on a curve. Finally he stopped, turned down his little lip and said, "I can't do it good."

Of course he could; he was doing just fine for his age. He just couldn't do what his big brother could. While there isn't much difference between forty-four and forty-seven, there is a lot of difference between four and seven.

And too often that's what we do. We judge ourselves against people who are older, wiser, and more experienced. I see this woman handling a life threatening illness like cancer and I can't even handle the flu without getting grumpy and complaining. One man sees another teach an outstanding class on Zechariah and he can't even give a decent five-minute Wednesday night talk. And both become so depressed they stop doing what they can do.

And if we aren't careful, instead of gradually growing and learning how, we give up too. Or we blame it on God for our lack of talent, or on our parents for not making us do our lessons as children, or for not taking us to church, or on the church for not using us as we "ought to be used," regardless of what we can and cannot do. Any of those is our handy alibi for sitting down and doing nothing.

The day that Judah complained was a Sunday. "Guess what?" I asked him.

His big blue eyes turned up to me as he said, "What?"

"Tomorrow is Monday and Silas will be at school. That means you can practice your scooter all day if you want to and before long, you will be as good as he is. And by his age, maybe even better!"

He gave me a lop-sided grin like he wasn't sure about that. "Really?" he asked.

"Really!" I said. And he hasn't given up. He knows he needs to work at it, but he also knows that he will get better. He already has.

And that's what we need to remember. Plus this: God doesn't compare us to brother or sister Whozit. He knows what we can and cannot do. He is the one who decides what we are capable of—not us! And if we keep on trying, we will "do it good," good enough to please a gracious Father.

> *So put away all malice and all deceit and hypocrisy and envy and all slander. Like newborn infants, long for the pure spiritual milk, that by it you may grow up into salvation— if indeed you have tasted that the Lord is good.*
>
> 1 Peter 2.1–3

42. Family Matters

It's fun watching them gradually realize that Grandma is Daddy's Mom and that Gran-gran is Daddy's Grandma, that Uncle is Daddy's big brother and Grandma is Gran-gran's little girl. Silas is beginning to figure it out, but Judah still gets a funny look on his face when you try to explain it. He raises those little eyebrows, cuts his eyes around and purses those lips—"And what have you been drinking?" he seems to think—except he wouldn't understand that either.

We want them to know who family is because family matters. We want them to understand that Silas's middle name may be the name of an apostle, but it is also the name of one of his great-great-grandfathers; that Judah's middle name may be the name of a great prophet, priest, and judge but it is the name of another great-great-grandfather as well. Even if they never knew those men, there is a connection.

Just look at the book of Obadiah. By the time it was written, few, if any, of the Edomites knew the Jews personally, but it still mattered to God that a long time before that Jacob and Esau had been brothers. He expected those two nations to treat each other like brothers.

> Because of the violence done to your brother Jacob, shame shall cover you, and you shall be cut off forever. On the day that you stood aloof, on the day that strangers carried off his wealth and foreigners entered his gates and cast lots for Jerusalem, you were like one of them. But do not gloat over the day of your brother in

the day of his misfortune; do not rejoice over the people of Judah in the day of their ruin; do not boast in the day of distress. Do not enter the gate of my people in the day of their calamity; do not gloat over his disaster in the day of his calamity; do not loot his wealth in the day of his calamity. Do not stand at the crossroads to cut off his fugitives; do not hand over his survivors in the day of distress. (Oba 10–14)

Because they did not help, because they "gloated" over their brothers' misfortune, because they actively stood in the way to prevent escape, God judged the Edomites and destroyed them. Their relationship with Israel was many generations removed, their people's knowledge of one another socially was small if at all, yet they were still expected to act like brothers.

So what does God think about siblings who argue over estates? About grudges that are held for decades? About bad feelings that are passed down to the next generation instead of being laid out of shame that such a thing exists in their hearts? God expects better of families, and why? Because that is the model for His people, the church.

The church is often described as "the household (family) of God," and that makes us brothers and sisters. God expects us to act like flesh and blood brothers and sisters. He expects us to love one another, not because we know one another, but because we are spiritually related—family. He expects us to forgive, to forbear, to help, to encourage and yes, even to admonish just as an older brother or sister would a younger one. It does not matter whether we "know" one another or not.

Let's add this quickly because someone is thinking it—yes, God even expects us to put His spiritual family ahead of our physical families; but assuming that is not an issue, my family life, even with the most distant of relatives, had better be a good one. How else will I know how to treat my brothers and sisters in Christ?

Do not rebuke an older man but encourage him as you would a father, younger men as brothers, older women as mothers, younger women as sisters, in all purity.

1 Timothy 5.1–2

43. The First Recital

I taught piano lessons (and later added voice lessons) for over 35 years. By the time I had to quit due to my eye problems, I had a full studio with a two year waiting list. My students participated in three competitions a year, and no less than four joint recitals, depending upon their ages and their pieces. At the end of the year, we had what I billed as "the Spring Program," because most people considered recitals "boring" and our programs were anything but. We put on a show and we had fun. And afterward I handed out sometimes as many as 20 awards, including some state competition trophies. Yes, it was a very big deal in our lives.

"Our lives" because my boys were part of it. I taught them both. Lucas went on to focus on voice and theory, while Nathan stayed with the piano. It's always satisfying to see your children follow in your footsteps. One day Nathan and I sat down and sightread duets for a half hour or so. I don't know about him, but I had a blast. He had grown and learned enough that we could share on an equal footing, a truly exhilarating experience.

And now, thanks to seeing Daddy play at home, my grandson Silas has started piano lessons. Last spring I went to his first recital. He had wowed me all morning, playing a hands-moving-together piece at a difficulty that no six-year-old student of mine had ever reached—with only eight months of piano under his belt. We not only practiced his piece, but his bow as well. (Any of my old students reading this will understand.) And so we all went to the auditorium and sat four rows from the front while he walked up to the grand piano and played his piece. Perfectly. With the classiest bow of the evening. The next year he did the same thing, this time playing three pieces—perfectly with an almost professional bow.

I couldn't stop smiling. And I also couldn't stop the tears from welling in my eyes. Somehow I managed to get them under control before he saw them, and I gave him a huge hug. "I am very proud," I said. "You have made me very happy."

As proud and happy as I was that day, there are a few other things that would make me even happier. I doubt I even have to list them. You know exactly what I am talking about because you wish them for your children and grandchildren too.

I still help Silas with his piano practice. With a new piece I often play the left hand while he plays the right, and then we swap places. By then he can manage to put both hands together himself. I still help with the theory homework, clapping out rhythms and asking questions that lead him to the right answers.

But more often than that, we talk about Bible characters, narratives and principles. We talk about God. We pray together and sing together. We memorize verses and recite them together. Doesn't he get this from his parents? Of course he does, but the more he gets from more different people—especially people who mean something to him—the more it will mean to him, and the better it will stick. Just like his Grandma and Daddy playing the piano.

That first recital was wonderful. But a first public prayer, a first sermon, and of course, the first commitment—when the time is right—will be even better.

> *But the steadfast love of the Lord is from everlasting to everlasting on those who fear him, and his righteousness to children's children, to those who keep his covenant and remember to do his commandments.*

> Psalm 103.17–18

44. Enough Monsters for One Day

Our dog Chloe is afraid of everything and everyone. The meter reader, the FedEx man, every repairman we have ever had, every visitor, and every family member, except my older son, all scare her to death. I have often wondered if we actually had cattle, whether this Australian Cattle Dog would be afraid of them, too.

What did all these people do to Chloe? Nothing. They simply exist in her world. So when Silas and Judah come to visit, she is extra terrified. After all, little boys are not still, quiet creatures. Not only are they in her world, they are in it loudly and rambunctiously. We will often tell her when our older son is on his way. She knows his name and when she hears, "Lucas is coming," she runs to the edge of the carport, faces the gate, and waits until he arrives, joyously running up to greet him. She does not know our grandsons' names. She thinks they are little monsters, though they are not at all. They are actually sweet little guys, but to her, in whatever language dogs speak, "monsters" is the name.

But there is one thing about this scaredy-dog: when we tell her Silas and Judah are coming "tomorrow," it doesn't bother her a bit. She still sits between us at the morning fire, relishing a head pat, a belly rub, and a tossed treat. The thought of the monsters coming doesn't keep her from enjoying today.

We need to be more like that. Jesus told us that in almost those exact terms. "Therefore do not be anxious about tomorrow, for tomorrow will be anxious for itself. Sufficient for the day is its own trouble [monsters]" (Matt 6.34). Handle today's problems today. Let tomorrow take care of itself.

Easier said than done, I know, but consider just two short things in the same passage. First, worry shows a lack of faith (v 30). God has promised to care for his people. He has promised to hear our prayers. He has promised he will never forsake us. No, he has not promised to fix everything exactly how we want it, nor has he promised we will never have trials and difficulties in life. But what he has promised will be far more help than worry ever could be. Trust him to help you and be with you through it all, and the monsters will be easier to bear. In fact, they might turn out to be as harmless as two little boys named Silas and Judah.

Second, only pagans should worry (v 32). Any time we fail to trust God and become so anxious that we can no longer even function, we are showing ourselves *not* to be children of God, but children of the Devil. "For *the Gentiles* seek after all these things, and your heavenly Father knows that you need them all" (Matt 6.32). Unbelievers have a father who doesn't care about them. You have a Father who gave His Son to save you. What would He *not* give you if you are faithful to Him?

Remember Chloe's lesson for you this morning. Take care of today. There are head pats and belly rubs and treats to be had—don't ruin them by worrying about the monsters of tomorrow.

Do not be anxious about anything, but in everything by prayer and supplication with thanksgiving let your requests be made known to God.

Philippians 4.6

45. The David Game

When I was a child we played several board games—Easy Money, Sorry, and Life usually, about the only things we had besides Checkers and Scrabble, which was our parents' game. Although my boys were more into playing outdoors, climbing trees, jumping off limbs on a Tarzan swing, and shooting the bad guys, whether robbers, Indians, or aliens, they enjoyed a board game occasionally, too.

So one year as I was trying to teach them the life of David, it suddenly occurred to me that learning that life might be a lot easier if it were a board game. So after a couple different versions were tried out, the Life of David game came into existence. I even used it in Bible classes.

This past spring, we kept our two grandsons for two full weeks. We have Bible lessons every night when they come to visit and as I was wondering what to teach this time around, I suddenly remembered that old David game. I wondered if, at 5 and 8, it might be a little too soon, but they sure showed me!

The first night I brought out the game and showed it to them. "Your daddy and your uncle used to play this," I told them, and instantly they wanted to also. "First, you have to learn about David, or you will never be able to play the game and win." Their only question was, "When can we start?"

I had already gone through 2 Samuel and the first three chapters of 1 Kings and divided it into 7 lessons, with 6 memory verses. I had drawn lesson sheets—questions with multiple choice "picture" answers, especially since Judah was just finishing up Pre-K this year—not that I needed to worry. He can read as well as I could in first grade! We did a lesson every night for a week, reviewing the previous lessons before starting a new one. After we did the seventh lesson, we spent time reviewing the memory verses cards. Finally, on the eighth night we were ready to play the game.

They loved it. We played it several times over the second week, letting that time be the "Bible lesson" for the day as they cemented facts and verses into their little heads. When it was time to go home, they wanted to take the game with them. That's how much they liked it, and I dare anyone reading this to quote those six memory verses and answer all of the 2 dozen questions involved in the game.

So how do you make your own? Well, I have no copyright on it, so let me tell you. If you can draw a straight line with a ruler and write legibly, you can do it, too. But your first task is to learn the life of David yourself. You will never be able to make an accurate game otherwise…

…So now that it's maybe a week or so later, and you know the life of David like the back of your hand, here is what you need: a standard sized piece of poster board, a black and several colored Sharpies, a straightedge, some card stock, and a pair of scissors.

1. First, take your poster board and draw a large square at what you have decided will be your beginning point, usually the bottom left hand corner, preferably in a bright color, and write "BETHLE-HEM" on it. Since David was born there, that is your "START."

2. Using your black Sharpie and the straightedge, begin drawing a switchback track around the poster board. The track should be about an inch wide.

3. Each "square" of the track should be about 1 ½ inches along the track. As you mark them off, write the various events of David's life and a "consequence" in the squares. For example: *Kill Goliath. Go ahead three spaces.* It's okay to have a blank spot here

and there. The boys called them "Safety Zones" because nothing bad can happen to you there.

4. Every half a dozen squares should be a "?" in a contrasting color. Obviously, if you land on that, you have to choose a question from the pile and answer it. (More about that in #9.) In my game, a correct answer lets you move ahead one space and an incorrect answer sends you back one. You can make it even more consequential if you want to.

5. Every five or six question marks should be an MV question (initials written down in the corner of the square), which means you have to do a memory verse from the memory verse pile. More about that in #10, but the same consequences of correct or incorrect follow.

6. Something a bit trickier here: David spent a lot of time running from Saul, particularly in Ramah and Gath, and he had a lot of trouble with the people of Ziph who kept telling Saul where to find him. So as I reached those particular portions of David's life, the board looked something like this: R ? A ? M ? A ? H. I did the same with Gath and Ziph. Do you see? It was a dangerous time, so there are more questions! I was also not afraid to put things like "Lose one turn" in those sections.

7. On the top and final line of the game, was a brief detour into the wilderness. That's where David once again had to flee when Absalom rebelled. So if you landed on the square that led to the wilderness, you had to take that detour. If your number safely sent you past it, you were lucky.

8. The final square of the game was a large blue "HOME." We talked about all of God's people trying to make it back "home" at the end of their lives by doing God's will and accomplishing his purpose for them. The boys got the point instantly.

9. Finally, go back and cut out smaller cards, about the size of those Chance Monopoly cards, and write your questions from the Life of David. Where was David born, Who was David's father,

How many brothers did David have, What job did David do for his father, and so on, all the way through his life, ending with, Which son rebelled, Which son tried to take over the kingdom while David was dying, and Which son became king after David died?

10. Now about those memory verse cards. When I taught the boys the six memory verses I had chosen—not all from Samuel, by the way, but all matching the evening's lesson in some way—I used the the Stick Man method previously discussed. By the time playing the game actually came around, those cards had been significantly reduced to one or two drawn images on much smaller cards that by then instantly evoked the verse in question. By the time Mommy and Daddy came home, those boys shocked them by what they had learned and what they could do, in spite of the fact that Daddy himself had done it as a little boy.

So, are you wondering how to teach your children about the Bible in a way that is fun, but very educational? Make your own Life of David game—or Life of Any Bible Character game for that matter. You might learn a little bit yourself.

For David, after he had served the purpose of God in his own generation, fell asleep and was laid with his fathers.

Acts 13.36

46. When Your Hero Has Feet of Clay

Here is an issue that arose with "The David Game," and if you use it, you may have this happen as well. In fact, this happens to everyone sometime or other in their lives. It just struck quicker as we were studying that great man of faith with our grandsons. As the first week of lessons wore on, you could see David growing into a *bona fide* Superhero in their eyes. Every day they eagerly awaited the next adventure.

Then we reached 2 Samuel 11. As I went through the narrative in terms I thought they could understand—David stealing both a man's wife and then his life—they became quieter and quieter. Their little blond heads dipped until their chins nearly touched their chests as they wrestled with the concept of a good guy who acted like a bad guy.

"Uh-oh," I thought. "Have I ruined everything?"

As it turns out, I hadn't. We were able to talk about good people making bad mistakes and how God always forgives and takes us back as long as we are truly sorry, willing to say, "I was wrong," and try our best not to sin again. Their spirits lifted. After all, they got in trouble now and again too, didn't they? Here was proof that they were still loved. David was once again a Bible hero.

The story of David—of Judah and Peter, too—is an inspiration and a warning to every Christian. No matter how well you have done for how long, you can still fall, but no matter how far you fall, God will take you back. "But if we walk in the light, as he is in the light, we have fellowship with one another, and the blood of Jesus his Son cleanses us from all sin" (1 John 1.7). We all hunger for that forgiveness and revel in its comfort.

Yet I have seen too many adults who, when they realize their heroes are not perfect, refuse to give that same forgiveness.

All children grow up thinking Mommy and Daddy are Superheroes. Sometime around middle school the luster begins to fade. By high school, parents are so often "wrong," in their eyes at least, that they can barely be tolerated.

And the truth is, parents are ordinary people. They do make mistakes, sometimes big ones. They have annoying habits and less than stellar character traits—*just like every other human on the planet.* The larger problem is they have children, sometimes grown children, who won't accept anything less than perfection.

When God tells us to forgive one another (Col 3.13 among a host of others), that goes for parents too, and any other person we have expected perfection from—mentors, teachers, preachers, elders, etc. We have no right to sit in judgment over their apologies, deciding whether or not they are sincere based upon nothing but our own arrogant expectations. We certainly have no right to ruin a relationship they might have with someone else. I have seen grandparents have no opportunity for a relationship with their grandchildren because their unforgiving children hold on to grudges from the past. Meanwhile, those same unforgiving children are making their own mistakes as parents because no parent does it all right—no, not even them, no matter what they might think otherwise. I have seen the same things happen to elders and preachers by an unforgiving congregant who spreads his ill will everywhere at every opportunity. Ruining another's perspective somehow validates his own.

Forgiveness isn't just for strangers or people we aren't particularly close to. The mistakes of a parent, mentor, or teacher may be more difficult to bear, but an unforgiving child or student or spiritual dependent is devastating to everyone.

> *Let all bitterness and wrath and anger and clamor and slander be put away from you, along with all malice. Be kind to one another, tenderhearted, forgiving one another, as God in Christ forgave you.*
>
> Ephesians 4.31–32

47. A Brave Little Boy

Just as I expected he would, Judah has long since conquered the scooter we gave him for his fifth birthday. In fact, he wore that one out and is now, at six, on the next size up. You should see that little guy as he rounds the cul-de-sac again and again, pushing off with his left foot, zooming around parked cars and navigating between the neighbor's trash cans on the edge of the road. His older brother on his bike can barely keep up.

No one has to remind him to put on his helmet. That's a good thing, because he has had his share of spills and the last time we were down, he had a doozy. We saw him hit the road, but he waved us off as he stood up and lifted the scooter off the road, pushing it all the way to the driveway. The blood was already pouring, so Granddad took him inside while I stayed with his brother.

After a few minutes I was told that I was needed. Granddad could do the cleaning, but Grandma was requested for the bandaging. When I sat on the floor in front of his dangling leg I got my first good look at that knee. A half dollar sized piece of skin was completely missing, as if someone had taken a grater and scraped it off, a nearly perfect circle. Bright red and oozing blood, I knew that it needed some sort of antibiotic and I knew it would hurt.

I looked up at those big blue eyes brimming with unshed tears, his little lips compressed into a straight line, trembling just a bit as he struggled to keep his composure. "I will use the spray and blow on it to make it hurt less, okay?"

"Okay," he managed to squeak out.

A quick spray and Grandma nearly undid herself blowing as hard and long as she could until the walls around us began to spin. Then a big bandage that barely covered that skinned spot and we were on to the next one, for the whole top of his foot and leg were scraped and bloody halfway to his knee. Altogether we used five bandages, but that little guy never uttered a peep.

"You were a very big boy!" I told him.

That seemed to ameliorate the still stinging wounds on his foot and leg. He gave me a small smile and he was off to play again. Later that evening when Mommy and Daddy came home, he was proud to show them his boo-boos and even prouder when I told them how brave he had been—"just like a grown up!"

It must have been a week later before the irony struck me. We told him how "big" and "brave" and "grown up" he had been. I am not sure why, because many of the grownups I have seen are perfectly happy to whine and fuss and demand attention from everyone about every little thing that comes along. Have you looked at Facebook lately?

Yes, some things do need the concern and care of others. Some things are so difficult to bear that we might very well topple without someone to lean on. Those things, which are far worse than a skinned knee, demand our love and help and attention.

But too many times a relatively minor trial is treated as if it were a life-threatening emergency. Too often a "skinned knee" is used to judge our brethren as uncaring, or to excuse ourselves from serving. Exactly what is "big, brave, and grown up" about that?

Let this sweet little boy, who did his best to be "grown up" teach you what it means to be brave and mature. Let him remind you that small things like skinned knees happen every day in the life of a Christian. God expects us to doctor the wounds and then get back up and carry on, to dry the tears and act like an adult. As a general rule, skinned knees won't kill you.

So we do not lose heart. Though our outer self is wasting away, our inner self is being renewed day by day. For this light momentary affliction is preparing for us an eternal weight of glory beyond all comparison.

2 Corinthians 4.16–17

48. Euphemisms

My little guys live on a cul-de-sac. And not just on it, but at the very end. Understand too, apart from one next door neighbor, no one else actually lives on the circle. The property around the rest of it is empty and meant by the builders to stay that way. That means they have the whole end of the street to themselves to play in.

And play they do, rounding the circle on scooters and bikes at speeds that ruffle the ends of blonde hair sticking out under their helmets and send their shirts flapping. It also means they have more room besides their front and back yards for Frisbee flying and ball playing and kite sailing. When we visit, more often than not, we wind up sitting on the front porch "spectating" while they play, their blue eyes bright and smiles big as they make turn after turn.

Reminds me of a place my family lived a few years before we moved to Tampa, another cul-de-sac called "Bristol Court." Only we lived at the top of the street, a hill by Florida standards, and I rode my own bike down that hill over and over. It may have been hot, but it was still a real breeze I felt in the middle of a Florida summer, cooling the perspiration for at least a few minutes as my bike picked up speed on the downward slope. The only difference between me and the boys? We called it a dead end street back then. If you had said "cul-de-sac", all of our neighbors would have looked at you with a "Huh?" look.

I suppose someone thought all those yellow signs that labeled a short street a "dead end" were insulting to the residents. First, they changed them to "No Outlet." Those signs are still up, but how many people now ever speak of their dead end street as anything but a "cul-de-sac?"

People are quick to use euphemisms, especially to put a better spin on something particularly ugly. "Ethnic cleansing" is really genocide. "Early retirement" often covers a company's downsizing by firing older workers. An "urban outdoorsman" is someone who is homeless. (Exactly how is that less heartless than "homeless"?) "Negative patient outcome" means he died! "Collateral damage" is also about death—the death of an unintended target. And yet more death—"pregnancy termination" is infanticide.

All of these things are attempts to make something that is uncomfortable to talk about, much easier to discuss, to deal with, and ultimately, to do. Satan has been doing this for a long time. "Let us take our fill of *love* till morning," the temptress says in Proverbs 7.18. What she means is, "Let's go commit adultery." In a day where love is supposed to excuse every sin, where "God knows my heart" takes the place of following His will and remaining "holy as he is holy," we must be especially cautious.

A cul-de-sac is a neat place to live and I am glad my grandsons have the same opportunity I had as a child to enjoy that safer street to play in. But here is something funny: the literal meaning of the French *cul-de-sac*, which is supposed to be some higher class word, we Americans think, is actually "the bottom of the bag." Which is right where we will find ourselves when we try to use more palatable words to cover up our sin before an angry God.

The bottom of the bag is still a dead end street for anyone who thinks otherwise.

Woe to those who call evil good and good evil, who put darkness for light and light for darkness, who put bitter for sweet and sweet for bitter!

Isaiah 5.20

49. Left Hand Practice

The last time we went to visit our grandsons, they had acquired a miniature Foosball game. About two feet long, each player had only two rods to handle instead of the usual four apiece. And that was plenty for rookie player Grandma. Both boys beat me soundly, but by the end of the weekend I was at least holding my own. Once I lost 9–7 instead of the customary shutout. Being older and thus more coordinated and better able to use strategy, nine-year-old Silas always beat six-year-old Judah. So I imagine it did Judah's little ego a world of good to beat up on Grandma!

Later that first day, I also helped with piano practice. (Nice to have a former piano teacher as a grandmother.) Silas is far more advanced than any student his age that I ever had, and it is a joy to listen to him. The way his little mind picks up instruction is another pleasure. After just a couple of thirty minute sessions, his playing was cleaner and his interpretation more mature.

Judah has just begun. His problem is confidence in his left hand. He showed me his method book and went through about 8 pages lickety-split, but always using only his right hand, even when the top of the page clearly showed the left hand fingers needed to play the bass clef notes. He even had to think backwards to get the correct notes played because, if you haven't noticed, your hand is a mirror image of the right. Your thumb is your first finger on each hand and the finger numbers go from there. So playing a note with the fourth finger of the left hand requires playing that note with the second finger of your right hand in order to play the correct note. Thinking backwards was easy for him, but he steadfastly refused to use his left hand. He may not have said it this way, but he clearly understood that his right hand was dominant and his left the off hand.

Whenever I suggested he try it with the left hand, he compressed his lips and shook his little head. Finally, this teacher of nearly forty years' experience figured out what to say.

"Do you remember how hard it was to play with your right hand the first time you started? But now that you have practiced it, your hand is stronger and you can do it much more easily, right?" I finally got an oh-so-slight nod. "So if you start using your left hand, it will get stronger, right?" No nod this time, but he was still listening. "And when your left hand gets strong too, you will be able to play Foosball better and maybe beat your big brother."

Now you could see the wheels spinning. "How about giving it a try?" I asked.

"I will sometime."

"How about if I leave for a minute?"

I didn't really get a nod, but I left the room and before five seconds had elapsed I heard the piano. He might have played a little more hesitantly than with the right hand, but that left hand played every single piece whether it was written for right or left hand. Do you know why that worked? I gave him some motivation that meant something to him.

Do you think God doesn't give us the same thing? You can find what my college Behavior Modification class called positive and negative reinforcement on practically every page of the Bible. From "in the day that you eat of it you shall surely die" (Gen 2.17) to "and he shall wipe away every tear from their eyes…" (Rev 21.4).

God finds the motivation that means the most to the people he is dealing with. Sometimes we seem to think that we should be doing things "just because" and that will make us better than anyone else. Please find for me any place that says that. Even when it seems that way, there is an unspoken prod somewhere in the context—gratitude, fear, love, *something* that will help us accomplish the task. Even Jesus was given motivation: "…who for *the joy* set before him endured the cross…" (Heb 12.2).

Sometimes we misinterpret the motivation. All those descriptions of Heaven as a place of magnificent wealth? God is not appealing to our greed. Remember who he spoke to. Those people understood what it meant to pray for their "daily" bread. They didn't have well-stocked pantries, grocery stores on the corner, bank accounts, life insurance, stock portfolios, or any other of the things we have. He was appealing to their desire for security. A place so wealthy that gold and jewels were used *as building materials and pavement* meant they would never have to worry about keeping their families fed and cared for. Walls so high meant they did not have to worry about Barbarians coming over the mountains to raid their villages.

As with all motivations, we hope to mature so that someday we can motivate ourselves with something a little less mundane. As our spirituality grows, so should the incentives we use to succeed. Someday I hope Judah will use his left hand at the piano so he can be a better pianist, and not just so he can beat his brother at Foosball. But for now? Whatever works.

Find what works for you. Don't be ashamed when you need a little help along the way. If you need a metaphorical Mt. Gerizim, find it. If you need a Mt. Ebal, give yourself a little tough love. Motivation is not a dirty word.

> *Bring the full tithe into the storehouse, that there may be food in my house. And thereby put me to the test, says the LORD of hosts, if I will not open the windows of heaven for you and pour down for you a blessing until there is no more need.*
>
> Malachi 3.10

50. The Guy in the Backseat

We were once again babysitting, this time in Tampa instead of here at home. Though I grew up there, that Tampa was long ago and far, far away. In fact, that night, a Wednesday, we headed for a place that forty years ago had been nothing but woods. Now it is a Chick-Fil-A, "where we go every Wednesday before church," we were told by our grandsons, and since Mom and Dad had been away for a week and a half already with three more days to go—and not just away, but on another continent—we wanted things to be like "normal," so off to that popular place we went.

Probably because I grew up in that area, even if it did look very different back then, my sense of direction was just fine when we came out after our meal. For one thing, I knew that turning left onto Fowler without a light, especially during the remaining minutes of rush hour, was a no-go.

"I wonder if there is a back way," I mused aloud.

Eight-year-old Silas immediately piped up from the backseat. "Turn right out of the back of the parking lot, go to the next street and turn right again." Of course he gets his superb directional skills from his grandma!

So I repeated his directions to Keith who could not possibly hear him from the front seat. He looked a little askance, but did as he was told. But then we came to 56th Street and by then, good old Granddad was totally turned around. He had no idea where he really was. I recognized immediately that though we needed to turn left, there was no break in the median there to do so. We would have to turn right, go to the Fowler light, and do a U-turn in order to be headed in the correct direction. And that light was not even a block down the street in the middle of thick traffic.

"Make sure you have enough room to get all the way across," I told him. "You will have to make a U-turn at the light to get to church."

"What are you talking about? A U-turn?"

"Yes, at the light."

"I don't want to turn there. It's the wrong place.

"No, it isn't. The church turn-off is behind us."

"Are you sure? It's just down a block or two on the left."

"No! You have to turn around. You have to make a U-turn at the light."

"But why do I want to do that?" he asked, thoroughly flum-moxed.

Once again the eight-year-old voice piped up from the back-seat. "Because that's how to get there," he said with simple logic.

At that point I laughed out loud. "Yes. That's how to get there."

"No it's not. I shouldn't have to make a turn at all."

"Yes, you do," and by then the car was in a bit of an uproar be-cause he was starting to pull out and the traffic was way too heavy for him to get all the way across into the left turn lane before he hit the light. "All the way, all the way, all the way!" the boys and I were shouting, and that is exactly what Keith did, having given up on his idea of where we were, though I think I still hear the echo of a horn and a screech of tires behind us as he did it.

As we sat there in our hard-won left lane, panting from half-fear and half-excitement, waiting to make a U-turn, Keith said very quietly, "What street is this?" and when I told him he added, "Ohh-hhh," with dawning realization. "Well, it's a good thing someone knew where we were."

And once again that little voice piped up from the backseat, "Always listen to the guy in the backseat." Then glancing over at his little brother he added, "On the right."

We have laughed at that story for a year and a half now. "Always listen to the guy in the backseat," one of us says, and then in unison, "On the right!" And the little guy had a point. When you are lost, when you don't know what to do, when you don't know where to go or who to turn to, ask "the guy in the backseat." In this case, that metaphor stands for someone who has been there, perhaps several times, as Silas had, someone who knows the ropes, someone who can lead you through the maze of possible routes safely to the other side.

Too many times we go to the wrong people. We go to the ignorant, the naïve, the ones who are in just as much trouble as we are. We steadfastly refuse to approach anyone who can really help us. And why? Could it be because we know we won't like the answer we will get? Could it be because it simply goes against the grain to let that particular person know we are having trouble? Could it be because, "No one really understands what it's like." Are we really that arrogant?

God created the church in his "manifold wisdom" (Eph 3.10), first, to hold forth the light of the gospel and save the world. But also so we can help one another, so we never have to fight the battles alone. Look around you some Sunday morning. You will see a group of people who, between them, have met almost every trial of life. You have a wealth of information and help at your beck and call, not to mention a raft of prayers going up daily if you only ask for them.

Sometimes your life is a crazy intersection at rush hour, with cars whizzing past and a left lane far across four lanes of that dangerous traffic, the very lane you need to be in to make a U-turn that might save your soul. Listen to the guy in the backseat and quit trying to figure it out alone.

Bear ye one another's burdens, and so fulfil the law of Christ.

Now we that are strong ought to bear the infirmities of the weak, and not to please ourselves.

Galatians 6.2; Romans 15.1

51. Gnats and Camels

Don't ever think that a seven-year-old doesn't listen to the conversation around him.

Judah probably heard it several times, the story of his great-grandfather's death, when his great-grandmother—Gran-gran—sat next to the bed and told her beloved just before he passed to wait for her at the gate. He heard it again at her funeral just before we sang "When All of God's Singers Get Home," when his uncle said, "I can imagine them walking through that gate hand-in-hand. Two of God's singers just got home."

That was two days before Thanksgiving, and a few days later he told his parents that he wanted to add something to his prayer list: that Gran-gran could find her husband in Heaven. He had never known "her husband," who passed almost exactly a year before Judah was born. Evidently he had imagined the scene and wondered how they could possibly find each other in the crowd and he didn't want Gran-gran to be scared and lonely. His daddy assured him that they had probably already found each other and were together again.

He continued asking questions about the man he never knew, so when he came for Christmas I asked if he would like to see some pictures. We had just gone through my mother's things and I had several at hand, from the seventeen-year-old high school graduate to the twenty-five-year-old Army draftee in Korea to the sixty-five-year-old gray-headed retiree, many with his sweetheart from high school days, Judah's Gran-gran. I told him that we all called him

Papa because that is what I had called my grandfather too. By the end of the session, he could point to even a picture from the 1950s and say, "There is Papa." Gran-gran's husband had become a real person to him, someone he was related to.

I was thinking about the preciousness of all of this when it suddenly occurred to me that I knew people who would have tsk-tsked me for telling my seven-year-old grandson that his great-grandparents were back together in Heaven. They would have pointed to stories in the Bible to prove that is not what life after death actually is—at least not yet. In fact, I can think of a few who would have accused me of lying to the child.

I recall at least three Biblical depictions of life after death. Each is different, and every one of them involve some sort of figurative language. Who are we to say that one or the other is the true and literal picture? God gave us those images to comfort us. Each has a point that makes us less afraid of death and more confident in our own destiny. As a parent or grandparent, God expects me to give my own children images they can relate to just as He did for His children. It isn't lying to talk about "waiting at the gate" any more than it is for God to tell us about streets of gold and gates of pearl or for Jesus to say, "I am the good shepherd," when he was actually a carpenter. I am simply following my heavenly Father's example in comforting my children.

Like the Pharisees, somewhere along the way we have missed the point of it all. We have, as Jesus cautioned, "strained out the gnats and swallowed the camel" (Matt 23.24). We have forgotten how patient Jesus was with the weak and the babes: "a bruised reed he will not break, and a smoldering wick he will not quench, until he brings justice to victory" (Matt 12.20). Instead we go plowing through the shrubbery heedless of anything but making our point and "being correct," when the whole point of figurative language is not to be literal at all.

A seven-year-old child is now comforted. As he matures in the Word he will come to know that what he was told was an image to help him understand and make him feel better. He will know that no, it probably was not exactly that way—those gates are figurative after all. But he will have learned the point in a way he will never forget: that God loves His children and plans to live with them forever, and that his great-grandparents are among those children. And, even better, he can be with them again one day.

> *But whoever causes one of these little ones who believe in me to stumble, it would be better for him to have a great millstone fastened around his neck and to be drowned in the depth of the sea.*
>
> Matthew 18.6

52. Childhood Memories

I am sitting here on the back porch of my children's new home, less than ten miles from the place I spent most of my remembered childhood. When I walk this yard with Silas and Judah, even the type of grass in it reminds me that I have come back home, and while I watch them play, the memories come flooding back.

The sun seems much brighter here than in north central Florida, where I have spent the majority of my married life. This may be only 120 miles further south toward the tropics, but I can barely stand to even look out the window without sunglasses on down here. I remember that bright sun reflecting off the pavement wherever we went. It almost made you wish for black tar roads—until you tried stepping on those barefoot and came away with something much worse than a sunburn.

The spring breezes down here are cool and pleasant, but without that underlying chill that demands a sweater at the ready just that little bit further north. We reveled in those almost perfect days when I was young because all too soon they were gone.

The summer heat is still that brutal slam when you step outside, but even so much closer to the coast here in Tampa, the humidity is less than that smothering blanket in the northern interior. I don't ever recall having to deal with pouring sweat at 8:00 AM As a child, I never felt like I might drown if I took too deep a breath!

And the clockwork arrival of a summer afternoon thunderstorm every day also came to mind. Gray clouds nearly as dark as night, lightning streaking across the sky, thunder like an explosion, winds that increased 20 or 30 mph and temperatures that dropped twenty degrees in mere minutes, followed by a deluge that had traffic pulling off the road to wait it out, and those unfortunate souls caught outside, drenched in only a few seconds.

I remember all these things from a childhood of walking three blocks to and from the bus stop, standing outside the locked school doors waiting after the bus had dropped us off and returned for a second route, raking up lawn clippings after my daddy mowed the yard, and swimming at a friend's "lake house." This may not look like the Tampa of my childhood, but the feel of this place hasn't changed a bit.

But the details? The traffic is thicker and louder. The outlying areas, including the trailer park where we spent our first year of marriage five miles "out of town," are more densely populated and congested. What used to be pastureland or strawberry and tomato farms is now subdivision after subdivision, "walled off" from the highway by a white board fence. As Thomas Wolfe said, "You can't go home again," but really, you can, if your memories are strong, if you can sit still and think and feel all those things from so long ago.

I find myself remembering my early years more and more lately. As good friends, some older but some exactly my age, pass on, those memories wake you up to what is really important. Now I can look back and realize that I had a great childhood.

No, it wasn't perfect. No, my parents did not do everything exactly right. Neither did I as a parent. But I am so grateful to them for teaching me right from wrong and respect for authority, for demanding I take responsibility for the things I said and did, for showing me how to keep on working until the task is done, for refusing to give in to pain, belittling comments from worldly acquaintances, and debilitating disease, but to keep on plugging for the Lord as long as you can draw a breath.

I am grateful that they made me go to church, do my homework, and even brush my teeth and clean my room. I love that they taught me to treat honesty as a lifestyle instead of a sometime convenience, and that I learned from them how to manage both my time and my money. I am grateful that I saw them respect others' opinions rather than running them down for doing things differently than they did and that they never thought the rules, even the unspoken ones, were only for everyone else. I was more than blessed in the age and place I grew up in to have parents who taught me to be color blind and to glorify God whenever an opportunity came to teach and/or help those who were different from us, and for showing me the examples of kindness and generosity, especially to the innocent and needy. And most of all, I am indebted to them for raising me to be a God-fearing, obedient servant of the Lord. I hate to think what my life would be like otherwise.

And then—what my children's lives would be like otherwise, and my grandchildren's. Don't ever think that what you view as a dull, routine life did not matter. Your children and your grandchildren and, should you live that long, your great-grandchildren will carry the memories you helped them make. It is gratifying that Silas and Judah will have memories a whole lot like mine, based not only on where they live, but *how* they live.

And it all started generations before them with simple people struggling through as best they could and, we hope, will continue on for generations to come.

> *As for man, his days are like grass; he flourishes like a flower of the field; for the wind passes over it, and it is gone, and its place knows it no more. But the steadfast love of the* LORD *is from everlasting to everlasting on those who fear him, and his righteousness to children's children, to those who keep his covenant and remember to do his commandments.*

Psalm 103.15–18

Flight Paths
A Devotional Guide for your Journey

When encroaching blindness took her music teaching career away, Dene Ward turned her attention to writing. What began as e-mail devotions to some friends grew into a list of hundreds of subscribers. Three hundred sixty-six of those devotions have been assembled to form this daily devotional. Follow her through a year of camping, bird-watching, medical procedures, piano lessons, memories, and more as she uses daily life as a springboard to thought-provoking and character-challenging messages of endurance and faith. 475 pages. $18.99 (PB)

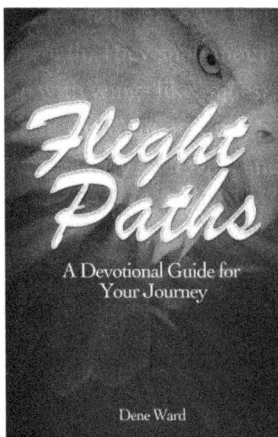

Soul Food
Lessons from Hearth to Heart

Cooking has always been a part of Dene Ward's life. She grew up in a house where they were always feeding someone and followed that same path as a wife and mother. On the table, she has always offered a nourishing meal; she now offers this collection to feed your souls, lessons from her hearth to your heart. 148 pages. $9.99 (PB)

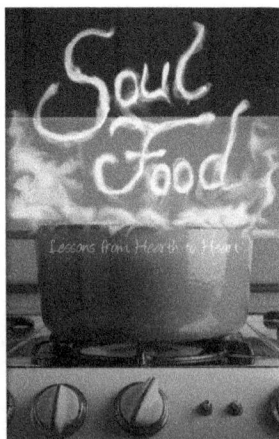

Down a Country Lane
...to a closer walk with God

Dene Ward was a city girl who married a country boy. They raised their family in the country, as their father was raised, and she quickly learned about toiling in the garden, chasing loose pigs, looking for snakes in the oddest places, and never taking for granted electricity, running water, and a clear path from the road to the house—half a mile down the country lane. Join her as she shares the lessons she has acquired with hard experience, which have also given her more insight to the rural-based lessons Jesus taught, and find yourself too, a little closer to God. 168 pages. $9.99 (PB)

In the Garden with God

Dene Ward and her husband Keith have gardened for nearly 40 years, which has shown her why God's prophets and preachers, including Jesus, used so many references to plants and planting—it's only natural. Join her for a walk in the garden with God. 142 pages. $9.99 (PB)

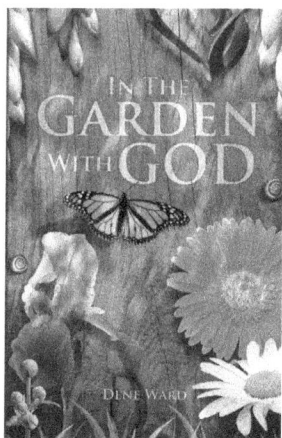

www.ingramcontent.com/pod-product-compliance
Lightning Source LLC
Chambersburg PA
CBHW031624040426
42452CB00007B/654